ENDORSEMENT FOR
THAT YOU MAY BELIEVE

I first met David in the student lounge of Grace Theological Seminary in the early fall of 1975. Living out his commitment to his Lord Jesus Christ, is his first priority.

David writes in a scholarly manner and in such a way that anyone reading his book can understand why Jesus Christ came to earth.

His book, *That You may Believe*, The Miracles of Jesus in the Book of John," is a tremendous resource for personal and group Bible Study.

I highly recommend his study of the Gospel of John. His teaching truly presents Christ as the Son of God and Savior of the world.
—**Ken Wooten**, M.Div, Grace Theological Seminary

***

That you may believe is book by Dave Staggers on 8 miracles of Jesus in Gospel of John. The title is taken from John 20:31, a summary statement on purpose of John's Gospel. Unlike the 3 synoptic gospels, Matthew, Mark and Luke, John's Gospel is different, as an apologetic gospel with a focus on enlisting faith in the reader using miracles as a main proof of Jesus deity. These miracles prove Jesus's deity and if one believes in Him as Lord and Savior, they also will gain eternal life by believing. It is just

that simple, unearned but as result of simple belief. This book is short and a good tool for evangelism and outreach. This approach is still desperately needed when so many books today are merely academic and not always helpful to the average person seeking to find simple faith in the Lord Jesus Christ. An easy read. Good for an evangelistic Bible Study, particularly with youth.
—**E. Ray Moore**, ThM. Grace Theological Seminary, Chaplain (Lt.Col.) USAR Ret., President and founder of *Frontline Ministries, Inc.* and *the Exodus Mandate Project*, author of *Let My Children Go*, *The Promise of Jonadab: Building a Christian Family Legacy in a Time of Cultural Decline*, executive producer of the film, *IndoctriNation* and contributor to the book, *IndoctriNation*

***

David Staggers offers a thorough examination of the miracles of Jesus in the Gospel of John, employing a clear and methodical approach to analyzing each miraculous event. He carefully unpacks the narratives, explores their theological significance, and highlights their broader implications. Staggers remains faithful to John's overarching purpose—demonstrating that these miracles not only authenticate Jesus' divine power but also affirm His identity as the Son of God. With accessible yet thoughtful insights, Staggers provides a compelling resource for those seeking to deepen their understanding of Jesus' miraculous works.
—**Rick Biesiadecki**, DMin., Midwestern Baptist Theological Seminary, Associational Mission Strategist, *Etowah Baptist Association, Woodstock, Georgia*

***

Every miracle in John's Gospel proves Jesus as the Son of God, that we might believe in him and receive life in his name. David Staggers thoroughly explains how each miracle serves that purpose while providing practical insight into what they mean for us today. Regardless of where you are in your spiritual walk—exploring faith, new to faith, or mature in faith—this book is for you.

—**James Griffin,** MDiv., Dallas Theological Seminary, Lead Pastor of Crosspoint City Church in *Cartersville, GA*, church planting network leader in *Metro Atlanta with NewThing and Engage Churches*. President of Engage West Africa

***

This book lives up to its title, *That You May Believe*: The Miracles of Jesus in the Book of John. David Staggers' treatment of the miracles of Jesus in the book of John is simply put--excellent. It is easy to read, yet contains a wealth of contextual information that helps the reader understand the significance of many of the details John includes in his account. I appreciate that he does not attempt to marshal naturalistic explanations to support the possibility that Jesus performed the miracle or how He did it. Staggers asserts that the reason John records 8 "signs" is because they were miraculous, supernatural events, thus proof to the people, and to us, that Jesus is who He says He is.

Staggers never loses sight of John's stated purpose (John 20:30-31) for choosing the signs he included in his gospel, "That you may believe that Jesus is the Christ, the Son of God." Staggers then explains his purpose for writing his book. "This is what we want to see in this study—how the miracles performed by Jesus show us who He is." The miracles were not recorded just to show us what Jesus could do, but to show us who Jesus is.

Other qualities of the book I loved were its devotional thoughts and practical challenges. Staggers emphasizes the meaning of belief is expressed in the term "believed in" Jesus. Believing in Jesus is not simply an acknowledgement of things about Him, even that He performed amazing miracles; it's the commitment of one's life in accordance with what they believe about Jesus and what He commanded us to do. I highly recommend this book; you may want to read it one miracle/chapter at a time, or you may find, like I did, that you don't want to put it down 'til you've finished it.

—**Ben Scripture**, M.Div. Grace Theological Seminary, Ph.D. Biochemistry University of Notre Dame, Teaching elder *Bethany Fellowship, Warsaw, Indiana.* Founder of *Scripture On Creation ministries*

THAT YOU MAY BELIEVE

The Miracles of Jesus in the Book of John

By

David P. Staggers

Published by KHARIS PUBLISHING, an imprint of KHARIS MEDIA LLC.

Copyright © 2025 David P. Staggers

ISBN: 978-1-63746-335-2

ISBN: 1-63746-335-9

Library of Congress Control Number: 2025940506

All rights reserved. This book or parts thereof may not be reproduced in any form, stored in a retrieval system, or transmitted in any form by any means - electronic, mechanical, photocopy, recording, or otherwise - without prior written permission of the publisher, except as provided by United States of America copyright law.

Unless otherwise noted, all Scripture quotations are taken from the Christan Standard Bible®, Copyright © 2017 by Holman Bible Publishers. Used by permission. Christian Standard Bible® and CSB© are federally registered trademarks of Holman Bible Publishers.

All KHARIS PUBLISHING products are available at special quantity discounts for bulk purchase for sales promotions, premiums, fund-raising, and educational needs. For details, contact:

Kharis Media LLC
Tel: 1-630-909-3405
support@kharispublishing.com
www.kharispublishing.com

I dedicate this book to my Lord and Savior, Jesus Christ, and to the Holy Spirit, who gave me insights for writing this book.

I also dedicate this book to my wife, Melodee, for her support through this project and her help in editing the manuscript.

Finally, I dedicate this book to my sister-in-law, Carol, for her editing skills, encouragement, and constructive feedback

Contents

Introduction xi

Chapter 1: The Uniqueness of the Gospel of John 15

Chapter 2: The Purpose of the Book of John 24

Chapter 3: Turning Water into Wine 37

Chapter 4: Healing the Royal Official's Son 50

Chapter 5: The Healing at the Pool of Bethesda 63

Chapter 6: Feeding the Five Thousand 77

Chapter 7: Walking on Water 90

Chapter 8: Healing the Man, Blind from Birth 101

Chapter 9: Raising Lazarus from the Dead 116

Chapter 10: The Resurrection of Jesus from the Dead 133

Chapter 11: Wrapping it Up 148

Appendix 1: Why Don't We See More Miracles Today? 164

Appendix 2: John 19:31-37 So That You May Believe 172

Bibliography 176

INTRODUCTION

One thing that I have not personally experienced in my many years of walking with Christ is a miracle. I have experienced a lot of circumstances where I saw the providential hand of God at work, but not a miracle. I am sure that some of you have experienced a miracle before, like an unexplainable healing from a health crisis. Yet, miracles are meant to be rare and not commonplace. If miracles were everyday today, then reading about the miracles described in the Bible would seem mundane and ordinary. But this is not the case today, particularly when we consider the miracles Jesus performed during His earthly ministry. It was an amazing, but relatively short period of time when He revealed Himself to the world with signs and wonders.

All four of the gospel writers included the miraculous works of Jesus in their accounts to demonstrate that He was who He claimed to be. Our focus in this book will be on the miracles that the Apostle John included in the Gospel of John. Jesus performed many miracles during His three years of public ministry, but John carefully chose only a few of the miracles to reiterate in his account. John was intentional in choosing these miracles and we want to be intentional in understanding why John picked these particular miracles.

This book is not intended to be a commentary on the passages to be examined. Commentaries tend to be a verse-by-verse description and explanation of the text. Instead, the focus of this work is on the important elements of the story which shed light on the miracles performed by Jesus. If questions arise after reading this book about the stories covered, I would suggest that you consult a good commentary to get your questions answered.

The inspiration to write this book came out of a small group study of the book of John, in which I wrote short accounts on the significance of each of the miracles recorded by John. It was from this effort that it seemed like a broader audience would benefit from this, if each of the miracles were examined in greater detail. Therefore, this book has two purposes in mind;

1. To gain an understanding of why John chose each of the miracles he included in the Gospel of John, and

2. To reveal practical insights that we can gain from the miracles. One thing I am very cognizant of when I make statements about understanding why John chose one miracle over another, is that I didn't personally know John and I didn't live during his era or in the part of the world where he lived. My Western, twenty-first century biases are going to come into play to some degree, but I am relying upon what John recorded and the Holy Spirit to guide me, as I draw my conclusions, based on my analysis of the miracles.

I trust this book will help you as we stop and look at each of the miracles John chose to highlight. As will be discussed in chapters one and two, John was not writing another historical account of Jesus's life. Like the other gospel writers, John had a purpose for his account that was more than just writing a biography. He wanted to show us who Jesus was and His purpose in coming into this world.

Chapter 1

THE UNIQUENESS OF THE GOSPEL OF JOHN

As a brand-new believer in Christ during my freshman year of college, I vividly remember being encouraged to begin my journey in the Bible with the Gospel of John. Since then, I have heard this same guidance given over and over again. New believers should begin reading the Bible with the book of John. In fact, I have even said it myself. The reason I typically give for starting with John is because it paints a clear picture of who Jesus is. It clearly shows both the divine and the human side of Jesus. For a new believer in Christ, the Book of John provides a strong foundation to build their faith. As you might guess, as a new believer in Christ, I followed the advice of my "spiritual father" and began with the Gospel John.

There are many ways we can approach the Book of John, but our focus in this book will be on the miracles of Jesus. Miracles (signs) were the focus of John and with intentionality he included a selected number of miracles in his narrative. Certainly, John did not include only miracles in his story of Jesus. There are other elements in John's book which makes it unique and different from the other gospel accounts. On the other hand, there are many elements in the other gospel accounts which are not included in the Book of John.

We get an overall sense of the book of John's importance and popularity when we recognize that John is the most published book of the Bible in a single-book format. There are other single-book books of the Bible that have been published, like Matthew, for example. By far, though, John has been the most published. This tells us that if we want someone to read only one book of the Bible, then it would be the Book of John.

The first four books of the New Testament (Matthew, Mark, Luke and John) are called the Gospels (good news) because they present to the reader the life of Jesus Christ. Each account of the life of Jesus is different, but Matthew, Mark and Luke have many similarities among them. These similarities among them are seen with the events they recorded about the life of Christ. In fact, many times they even make the same statements. This is not to say they are being redundant, but they are presenting their stories from different perspectives. Matthew's perspective was being an eyewitness to the events. Mark recorded the events as recounted by Peter. Finally, Luke investigated and recorded the events after interviewing eyewitnesses.

Matthew, Mark and Luke are commonly called the Synoptic Gospels. They are Synoptic Gospels because there are so many similarities among them. There are many places where there is word-for-word agreement among them. The idea of synopticism is, "…presenting or taking the same or common view"[1], as witnessed in these Synoptic Gospels.

To get a sense of how unique John's account was, we find that… "the material that John's gospel has in common with one or more of the Synoptic Gospels amounts to only 8% of the FG [fourth gospel]"[2]. This means that 92% of the content in the Book of John is unique. Some examples of John's unique material include the extensive discourse Jesus had with His disciples and His prayer found in John 14-17. Another example is John's unique beginning to his gospel, describing the deity of Jesus before He took on flesh and lived among us (John 1:1-5). Even though most of John's account does not have common content with the Synoptic Gospels, there is a common focus among all of the gospel narratives on the last week of Jesus's life. Again, John presents a unique account of the last week of Jesus's life, but all of the Gospel authors understood the importance of the death, burial and resurrection of Jesus Christ. This is clearly seen by the focus their narratives had on these events. These actions are the climax of Jesus' time on earth, culminating in His sacrifice on the cross, for the sins of the world, and then rising from the dead three days later.

Unlike the other gospel accounts (Matthew, Mark and Luke), the Gospel of John approaches the life of Christ in a different way. John's intent was not to write another biography of the life of Jesus Christ, but to highlight key events and interactions in His life. John also provides some chronological references of Jesus' life, which the other gospel accounts do not. John's intention for doing this was to help provide his audience a framework for when these events took place. For example, John has a lot of his narrative revolving around Jesus's ministry in Judea when Jesus attended different festivals in Jerusalem, like the Passover event. These references have helped us to understand the length of time that Jesus's public ministry lasted, which is not clear in the other gospel accounts. Therefore, I should make it clear, at this point, that none of the gospel writers were trying to write a biography of Jesus in the strictest sense of the word though. Typically, biographies are intended to record the events of a person's life in chronological order and include an understanding of the person. Hence, the gospel writers were more intent on recording the events of Jesus life to show us who He is and His purpose for coming to the earth.

Although John was written over two decades later in the A.D. 90s, the Synoptic Gospels were written before the fall of Jerusalem by the Romans in A.D. 70. This alone makes the audience of John different from the writers of the Synoptic Gospels. The audience of John was second and third generation Christians and predominantly Gentiles. By the time of the writing of John, there were very few first-generation Christians still alive. This means that John's readers were further removed from the actual events. Think back in your own life about the events that took place sixty years before. For most of you reading this, you were not even born, therefore, more detailed explanations would be needed to describe those events. With the Book of John written in the A.D. 90s, he had to provide more detail in his narrative because his audience was not from the region where Jesus lived and ministered and they would not be familiar with the region and the culture. This helps to explain the details you see in some of John's accounts which are not seen in the Synoptic Gospels. Also, John was an eyewitness to most of these events as we see in the details he included in his narrative. One good example of these unique details is found in John 18:15-16; "…Simon Peter was following Jesus, and so was another disciple. Now that disciple was known to the high priest, and entered with Jesus into the court of the high priest, but Peter was standing at the door outside. So, the other disciple, who was known to the high priest, went out and spoke to the doorkeeper, and brought Peter in." John was that "other disciple" mentioned in these verses and we learn that he had special access to the proceedings of Jesus' trial because the high priest knew him. Also, John was the only disciple of Jesus who personally witnessed His crucifixion. Jesus even talked with John while on the cross (see John 19:26-27).

It is generally agreed that John wrote his narrative of Jesus from the city of Ephesus in Asia Minor. One of the late second century church fathers, Irenaeus, confirms this stating, "afterwards, John, the disciple of the Lord, who also had leaned upon His breast, did himself publish a Gospel during his residence at Ephesus in Asia" (Against Heresies, 3.1.1). The "afterwards" that Irenaeus is referencing to, are the other gospel accounts. In other words, he is confirming that John was written after the other gospels had been written. Irenaeus also gives us a general timeframe of when John wrote his gospel. Ephesus was the city of residence for John in the latter days of his life, pointing us to the A.D. 90s as the time when the Book of John was written.

Perhaps the most outstanding characteristic which makes the book of John unique is the emphasis on the deity of Christ. His focus on Christ's deity reflects the environment in which John was writing where misconceptions were already emerging about the person and work of Jesus Christ. We immediately see John addressing this in the first verse of the book, "In the beginning was the Word, and the Word was with God, and the Word was God." The first five verses of John 1 describe His divinity and this became the foundation for the rest of the book where Jesus demonstrates His deity through words and deeds. Jesus clearly made claims about His divinity over and over throughout the book. The most outstanding example was in John 8:58 where He said, "Truly, truly, I say to you, before Abraham was born, I am." The use of this phrase "I am" was pointing to the Old Testament name of God which God revealed to Moses in the burning bush (see Exodus 3:13-14). The religious leaders understood what Jesus was saying by their extreme response, "Therefore, they picked up stones to throw at Him…" (vs. 59). Jesus proved His deity through miracles. He showed that only a creator, God, could perform miracles. The nature of miracles will be explained in the next chapter to show that miracles can only be divine acts.

Miracles in the Book of John

As mentioned in the Introduction, this book is not intended to be a commentary on the Book of John, The focus of this book is on the miracles of Jesus, because John focused on specific miracles which were intended to be signs to Jesus's audience. John had a huge number of miracles to choose from, during the ministry of Jesus, but he picked only a few to highlight. John picked these miracles with a specific purpose in mind. This will be discussed in the next chapter.

The miracles recorded in the book of John are:

- Turning the water into wine (John 2:1-11)
- Healing the son of the royal official (John 4:46-54)
- Healing the lame man at the Pool of Bethesda (John 5:1-17)
- The feeding of the 5,000 (John 6:1-14)
- Jesus walking on the water (John 6:15-21)
- The healing of the man blind from birth (John 9:1-41)

- Raising Lazarus from the dead (John 11:1-46)
- The resurrection of Jesus and His appearances to His disciples (John 20:1-9; 26-29)

Some commentators also include the huge catch of fish in John 21:1-11 and the cleansing of the temple court found in John 2:13-22. I have not included these events in our examination of the miracles in John. I will explain the reasons for this in the next chapter.

In summary, even though the book of John is uniquely different from the Synoptic Gospels in terms of content, it does not contradict what the Synoptics have recorded. In fact, all of the gospel accounts complement one another. John did not write about most of the events described in the Synoptic Gospels, but fills in some of the gaps that are not present. For example, a small gap that John covers, is the timeframe for the miracle of the feeding of the 5,000. This event was recorded by all of the gospel writers, but John includes in verse 4 of chapter 6, this small detail, "…now the Passover, the feast of the Jews, was near." John gives us the timeframe when this event took place. It occurred in the spring during the beginning of the barley harvest.

The four gospels were written by four authors, providing four perspectives on the life of Jesus, with each emphasizing specific aspects of His life. We have seen some of the unique elements of the Book of John, but John, unlike the other gospel writers, tells us specifically why he wrote the book. He included a purpose statement in the book which we will examine next and see how it impacted the structure of his book.

---

[1] "Synoptic". https://www.merriam-webster.com/dictionary/synoptic. Accessed 5/27/24.

[2] Murray Harris, John in *Exegetical Guide to the Greek New Testament* (Nashville: B&H Publishing, 2015), p. 6.

Chapter 2

THE PURPOSE OF THE BOOK OF JOHN

Most of the time, when I plan to read a non-fiction book, I will read the introduction to the book first. The introduction will give me a sense of what the book is about and the perspective the author is planning to present in the book. In other words, the author will state his/her purpose/thesis in the writing of the book at the beginning of their work. It is usually stated in the introduction or the first chapter, as the author explains why he wrote the book and what he hopes to show his audience, as they read the book. This is really helpful for the reader to know what the book is all about and what the author wants us to gain from the work.

The apostle John took a different approach and included his purpose statement towards the end of his book. He decided to have his audience read almost the whole gospel account before telling them why he wrote the book. It makes sense, if you were placing your purpose statement at the end of the book, that it would be your concluding remark for the reader. Then the reader would have the opportunity to reflect upon what they just read. In this case, John chose to include his purpose statement at the end of chapter twenty instead of at the end of the book (chapter 21). It appears that John chose to place his purpose statement at the end of chapter twenty as a response to the remark Jesus makes to Thomas in verse 29. "Because you have seen Me, have you believed? Blessed are they who did not see and *yet* believed." John begins verse 30 with the conjunction, *therefore*, based upon what Jesus told Thomas in verse 29. John's focus is on believing, even though you have not personally witnessed the resurrected Jesus. This leads to the purpose statement of John in verses 30-31.

John's Purpose Statement

In John 20:30-31, the apostle John states, "Therefore many other signs Jesus also performed in the presence of the disciples, which are not written in this book; but these have been written so that you may believe that Jesus is the Christ, the Son of God; and that believing you may have life in His name." In these verses, John clearly states his purpose for writing this book. His purpose was not to write a biography as a historical record for posterity, but to highlight a number of signs (miracles) in the life of Jesus. The other gospel writers (Matthew, Mark, and Luke) had already written accounts on the life of Jesus and John did not need to repeat what had already been written. John's desire was for the reader to come to faith (believe) or continue in their faith, based on the evidence that Jesus is in fact the Messiah and God in the flesh. John continues on to give his readers the assurance that continued faith (believing) in the name of Jesus results in life (eternal life).

In addition, John was deliberate in picking out the miracles he wanted to include in his gospel account, and he had a lot to choose from. John 21:25 makes this very clear. He picked the signs he thought would have the most impact in bringing the reader to faith in Christ. In the following chapters of this book, we will carefully investigate each of these miracles to see why John chose them and how they give us insights into Jesus as the Christ, the Son of God. In the previous chapter, these particular signs were highlighted; therefore, there is no need to highlight them here. We will continue to examine the highlights of John's purpose statement, as follows.

To Show He is the Christ

John tells us that the purpose of the signs is that you may believe that Jesus is the Christ. What does John mean by the title, Christ? First of all, we know it comes from the Old Testament, where the Hebrew word for Christ is Messiah. Both of the words mean anointed one and describes a person sent by God to deliver His people from their sins. The connection between Christ and Messiah is clearly made by John in two places where the speakers, Andrew and the Samaritan woman, declare that Jesus is the Messiah, and then John includes the phrase, "...that is, the Christ" (see John 1:41; 4:25).

In the New Testament, the idea of Jesus being the Messiah was clearly demonstrated to the point that the title "Jesus Christ" or "Christ Jesus" is found approximately 210 times. Out of that number, it is found only five times in the Gospels because the Gospels were showing their readers that Jesus was the Christ prophesied in the Old Testament, whereas the rest of the New Testament was affirming that He was the Christ. This tells us that the words, *Jesus* and *Christ*, are intimately tied together to the point that some have thought that Christ is Jesus's last name! It is not His last name, but it does describe who Jesus is. The early church clearly understood that Jesus was the Christ, as described in the Old Testament.

Even though the New Testament writings had been firmly established and distributed by the time John wrote his Gospel sometime in the A.D. 90s, there were also forces at work to dispute or undermine the claims of Jesus as the Christ. On one side were the Jews who were dispersed throughout the Roman Empire. They argued that Jesus was not the Messiah because He did not fit their criteria for being the Messiah. We see John include this issue in the Gospel of John when some of the Jews said He could not be the Messiah because He is from Galilee and not from Bethlehem (John 7:41-42). These

Jews did not know nor understand that Jesus was born in Bethlehem and fulfilled the prophecy of Micah 5:2.

On the other side was a heretical group called the Gnostics, who mixed Christianity with pagan philosophy. They believed there was a secret knowledge about Jesus that could only be known by associating with them. There was no unified teaching from the Gnostics, but when it came to Jesus, many of them taught that He did not exist in the flesh but was only a spirit that appeared as human on the earth. John addressed this wrong teaching early in his Gospel by showing his readers that Jesus was God (John 1:1) and then telling them that Jesus became flesh and dwelt among us (1:14). The church historian, Kenneth Latourette, summarizes well the distorted view that the Gnostics had of Jesus. "Gnosticism tended to minimize the historical element in Christianity and to divorce the faith from the life, acts, teaching, death, and resurrection of Jesus of Nazareth"[1]. On the other hand, John showed his readers that Jesus was a real person who lived and ministered in a real world.

John addressed both the Jewish and Gnostic views of Jesus in his account to show that Jesus was the Christ as described in the Old Testament and that He was God in the flesh. The signs which Jesus performed verified His claims and His teachings. It was in an environment like this that John wrote the Gospel to challenge and correct these false teachings.

What Does John Mean by Signs?

The signs performed by Jesus were critical to refute the Jews and the Gnostics and lead the reader to believe that Jesus is the Christ. When we look at the "signs" John highlights in his gospel account, we see the signs are in fact miracles. The word for sign (Gr: *sēmeion*), is used seventeen times in the Book of John. In the context of each of these verses, it is clear that the verses are referring to miracles as being the signs. In fact, at the end of the first miracle recorded by John, Jesus turning the water into wine, John states, "This beginning of *His* signs Jesus did in Cana of Galilee…" (2:11). He clearly identifies the miracle as being a sign.

John was intentional in using the word 'sign' instead of miracle because of the meaning of the word. *Sēmeion* has a range of meanings, but in the context of John, the word is used in the sense of providing proof and authenticating the person performing the sign. Spicq states, "This is how St. John sees miracles: they authenticate Jesus as the Messiah announced by the prophets. They are above all a sign of the Father's favor…"[2]. John is making the point in using the word 'sign' that Jesus's miracles were intentional to prove who He is. Even one of the rulers of the Jews recognized this. Nicodemus, when he came to Jesus at night, introduced the conversation with, "Rabbi, we know that You have come from God *as* a teacher; for no one can do these signs that You do unless God is with Him" (3:2). In other words, the miracles of Jesus were proof to the people that He is who He says He is. This is what we want to see in this study--how the miracles performed by Jesus show us who He is.

The Significance of the Word "Believe" in John

The central point of John's purpose statement is the word "believe". John had two audiences in mind when writing his gospel narrative. He desired that the unbeliever reading this story would believe that Jesus was indeed the Christ. John also desired for the follower of Christ to continue in his belief. The Greek word for "believe" is *pisteuō* and this word occurs 98 times in the book of John. You immediately get the sense that this word is an important part of his narrative based upon the number of times it is used. The word, "believe", can be used as a verb or a noun and John uses the verb form exclusively in his gospel account. Verbs are used for expressing action or a state of being and John predominantly uses the verb form of *pisteuō* as an action verb. In other words, belief does not come passively, but is an action we must take. In the context of John's purpose statement, he is presenting the gospel signs which point us to Christ. Thus, as his readers, we should act upon these signs with belief.

John also reinforces his use of the word, 'believe', with the preposition, "in" (Greek: *eis*). Using it as an idiom, John says, "…believe in…" This idiom speaks of a divine object of faith, not a human object of faith[3]. John uses this phrase thirty-six times in his gospel account. To illustrate this, let's look at a familiar verse--John 3:16. "For God so loved the world, that He gave His only begotten Son that whoever <u>believes in</u> Him shall not perish, but have eternal life." I underlined the phrase under discussion. In this verse, we are able to see Him as the object of belief. In the context of the verse, the "Him" is referring back to Jesus, God's only begotten Son. Harris states, "This distinctive prep. phrase "believe in" depicts the total committal of one's total self to the person of Christ as Messiah and Lord, something more than an intellectual acceptance of the message of the gospel and the recognition of the truth about Christ, although these aspects are involved"[4]. As we investigate each of the signs in the book of John, we will recognize that believing does not necessarily mean a mature faith as an outcome, but is the starting point for growing in our commitment to Christ.

As we read the Book of John and examine the signs, we will also pay special attention to whether this Johannine idiom, "believe in," is used. We will also discuss its significance in the context of each passage being examined.

Even though we are 2,000 years removed from the miracles recorded in John, these miracles still have the same purpose and impact they did with John's original readers, as it has on us. The miracles point us to who Jesus is, in order that we might believe. More than that, the result of believing in Him is still just as true today as when John first wrote these words, "...that you may have life in His name." That is the power of the gospel and the finished work of Christ on the cross. The gospel still has the same power and efficacy as it did when these events originally occurred.

David P. Staggers

Miracles and the Providence of God

Before we consider the specific miracles that John included in his gospel account, we want to be clear about what constitutes a miracle. The biggest issue we see with identifying miracles is confusing a miracle with the providential hand of God. In our culture today, we tend to throw around the term "miracle" rather freely. We will speak of minor events that are surprising to us as a miracle. Definitions are important and understanding the difference between a miracle and providence is important. We will start off by defining a miracle. A miracle is an act of God through which he suspends or changes the laws of nature to accomplish His will. There are two important elements in this definition: (1) God is the author of the miracle and (2) He suspends or changes specific laws of nature. This means that God, the One who created the laws of nature, can do whatever He wants with the laws of nature. We must not forget that God uses human instruments to do miracles, but God is still the One who is doing the miracle. This is important to note so that we do not attribute special power to certain figures in the Bible, like Peter and Paul, who performed miracles in the New Testament. It was God who was at work through them.

Let's look at an example of a miracle in Luke 17:11-19, when Jesus healed the ten lepers. Jesus told the ten lepers to show themselves to the priests and "…as they were going, they were cleansed" (vs. 14). The text is not clear how the lepers were cleansed, but clearly Jesus was the one who healed them. Jesus did not touch them, or give them some medicine, or even tell them to do something. Their leprosy completely went away as they were going to the priests. That was the point of Jesus sending them to the priests. The priest was the only person in their culture who could call a leper clean and allow them to enter back into the society. There is no natural explanation for the leprosy to immediately go away other than Jesus caused it to disappear. In other words, it was a miracle. God was the author of this miracle and physiological processes were reshaped to cause the lepers to be immediately healed. We know Jesus altered the processes because even with today's medical treatments, leprosy can only be healed with a regimen of medicines over a six-to-twelve-month period, depending on the type of leprosy afflicting the patient.

Let us now contrast miracles with the providence of God. As mentioned above, with a miracle, certain laws are temporarily changed or suspended to accomplish His will. With providence, God orchestrates events to accomplish His will. The laws of nature are not manipulated contrary to their established function, but God operates within the realm of the natural universe to accomplish His will.

An excellent example of God's providential hand at work was an event often called, "Miracle on the Hudson." This event occurred on January 15, 2009 when Capt. Cheasley "Sully" Sullenberger successfully landed a passenger jet on the Hudson River in New York City when both engines lost power after being struck by a flock of birds. He was not able to return to the airport to land, therefore, he had to glide the plane in for a landing on the river. All 155 passengers and crew survived the landing. Whereas, this event was amazing and we can see the hand of God at work in this, it was not a miracle. God operated within the realm of the natural universe to create the right conditions for the plane to land. These conditions include the skill set of Sully, the weather conditions and the timing of the bird strike to allow Sully to guide the plane to a safe landing. This was an improbable landing, especially with no loss of life, and many acknowledged the hand of God in directing this landing. Therefore, it is still called "Miracle on the Hudson" to this day.

By far, we experience God's providential hand at work much more often than God working through a miracle. Many times, however, we miss seeing God's hand at work because we are not "tuned in" spiritually or we attribute the event to good fortune. In the case of miracles, many people miss God's hand at work because of unbelief. They either explain away the miracle as not happening or attribute it to natural causes. This was the way it was in Jesus' day and that is how it is today. Many, many people witnessed the miracle and yet they did not believe it. This was especially true of the Jewish religious leaders. In fact, their response to the miracles of Jesus was to plot among themselves on how they could kill Him (see John 11:53).

John's intent for the miracles highlighted in the Gospel of John was to clearly attribute the miracles to Jesus so as to lead people to have belief in Him. John wrote this account of Jesus' life in the latter part of his own life; therefore, he had plenty of time to reflect on which signs should be included in his narrative. Anyone could make the verbal claim that they were "the Christ" and there were some who did make this claim during this era. Miracles, however, provided the avenue for validating this claim and John chose miracles that validated over and over that Jesus was indeed the Christ the Jews were looking for.

In the previous chapter, I mentioned that some commentators included a couple of events in the life of Christ as miracles. These were the huge catch of fish in John 21:1-11 and the cleansing of the temple court found in John 2:13-22. I am not including the cleansing of the temple by Jesus because it does not meet the definition of a miracle. Jesus's act appears to be merely a human act, with perhaps the providence of God involved in seeing the temple court cleared. It is a fantastic act for one person to accomplish, but it does not elevate to the level of being a miracle.

The second event was the huge catch of fish that occurred in John 21, when Jesus told the disciples to throw their net in the water on the right side of the boat. This was after all their previous efforts to catch fish had failed. John was so amazed by this act that he included details like the specific number of fish caught and highlighted that despite the massive catch, the net did not break (vs. 11). Was this a miracle or the providence of God? It appears to be the providence of God in bringing together this large school of fish to the very place where the net was to be thrown into the water. There is no evidence or reason that God would have to alter the laws of nature to make this happen. It was His divine hand at work.

Purpose of this book

Unlike the apostle John, I will tell you the purpose of this book, at this point, rather than wait until the end. When we consider the signs (miracles) that John included in his account, we should look at these miracles in the light of John's purpose stated above. In other words, how does each of the miracle narratives contribute to his purpose statement? This is the reason for writing this book. We are going to analyze each of the miracles John has included in his book and gain insights into how each miracle points to Jesus as the Christ.

As stated before, John was writing to a first-century audience, but what he wrote is equally applicable to us in the twenty-first century. We will consider how each of these miracles helps us understand today who Jesus is, with the goal of either seeing the reader come to faith in Christ or for the believer in Christ to experience growth in Christ.

---

[1] Kenneth Lattourette, *History of Christianity, Vol. 1* (Peabody, MA: Prince Press, 1975), p. 125.

[2] Celslas Spicq, *Theological Lexicon of the New Testament, Vol. 3* (Peabody, MA: Hendricksen Publishers, 1994), p. 253.

[3] Murray Harris, John in *Exegetical Guide to the Greek New Testament* (Nashville: B&H Publishing, 2015), p. 31.

[4] Ibid, p. 32

Chapter 3

Miracle #1 in the Book of John
Turning Water into Wine

When we start a new job, we want to create the right impression about ourselves to those around us. We want to convince them that we are the right person for the job. We recognize that how we initially perform will have a positive or negative impact as we move forward. This was certainly the case with Jesus as He was beginning His public ministry. He launched His ministry with His baptism by His cousin, John the Baptist, and it was endorsed by the Holy Spirit descending upon Him as a dove (John 1:32). When Jesus started recruiting disciples, as described in the latter part of chapter one, it was necessary to show them He was the Messiah (Christ) as prophesied in the Old Testament. To validate His claim as Messiah, Jesus needed to show them a sign that was convincing enough for them to believe.

Setting the Scene

That first sign (miracle) which Jesus performed was also the first sign that John documented in chapter two. In verses 1-11, he records the story of Jesus turning the water into wine at the wedding He attended in Cana. This miracle had a subtlety to it because Jesus intended for only a few people to witness it. The miracle was not a public sign nor a private sign done in a secret place. It was designed for a specific audience with a particular purpose in mind. This selected group was His mother, His disciples, and the servants who filled the waterpots. Indeed, others became aware of the miracle after it happened, but they were not witnesses to the actual event. (Aside: Can you imagine the reaction of the bridegroom when he was told about this new batch of wine?)

A Jewish wedding during the time of Jesus was an elaborate affair which lasted over several days. There was lots of feasting with many attendees coming and going. This meant a lot of wine was consumed. This is not to imply that these wedding celebrations were drunken affairs but it does imply that a lot of people were invited to this wedding. It is likely that Jesus and His disciples did not arrive at the wedding on the first day of the celebration, because by the time they arrived the wine had run out.

When reading the text, it seems strange that Mary specifically tells Jesus, "They have no wine" (vs. 3). She states this with the implied expectation that Jesus can fix the problem. Even though the text does not tell us, it appeared that Mary recognized that Jesus's time to make Himself known to the public was near, if not now. Don't forget what Mary had experienced with her son for the past thirty years. She had a clear sense His time had come to reveal Himself to the world. This recognition of her son's imminent public disclosure was so clear to her, she was not deterred by Jesus's response, but simply told the servants, "Whatever He tells you, do it" (vs. 5).

The Vessels Used for the Miracle

The vessels that were used for holding the water, which was turned into wine, were described by John with some detail. John tells us the type of vessels they were, the number of vessels, and the size of the vessels. The vessels were waterpots and they were large enough to hold two or three measures of water. The sidenote of your Bible probably tells you a measure (Gr: metrétés) is equivalent to 39.39 liters or 8.75 gallons. Therefore, John is saying each waterpot holds between 17.5 and 25.25 gallons of water. John allows us to do the math and figure out that the six waterpots could potentially hold between 105 and 151.5 gallons of water. The point being made by John is that the waterpots could hold a lot of water.

There is one other point to note on the size and number of the waterpots. John tells us that Jesus commanded the servants to fill all of the waterpots and they "…filled them up to the brim" (vs. 7). In other words, Jesus turned between 105 and 151.5 gallons of water into wine. This gives us a sense of the magnitude of the miracle Jesus performed. To put some perspective on this, wine, today, is bottled and the typical volume of a wine bottle is 750ml. If we convert this to the volume of water Jesus turned into wine, it would be equivalent to between 530 and 764 bottles of wine.

John gives us two other important details about the waterpots. The waterpots were made of stone and their purpose was, "...for the Jewish custom of purification" (vs. 6). These two details are tied together because stone was considered the best material to use for waterpots to avoid defiling the water in the pots. In other words, wood or clay pots would be subject to contamination because wood and clay are more porous. This is relevant to the purpose of the waterpots: for purification. John specifically describes the custom as being Jewish and not Levitical. In other words, this practice was developed by the Jews and was not a practice described in the books of the Law. We gain an insight into the use of these purification waterpots in Matthew 15:2 and Mark 7:2 where the Jews complain to Jesus about His disciples eating bread without washing their hands. This was a problem, as the Pharisees described it, because they were not "...holding firmly to the tradition of the elders" (Mk. 7:3). Apparently, the waterpots in the John passage were being used to allow the guests to ceremonially cleanse their hands before eating. Jesus repurposes the waterpots from accommodating a tradition of man to be used for the glory of God.

Insights from the Miracle

This miracle did not show Jesus in all of His glory and power, but the miracle gave the disciples an insight into who He is. Jesus showed them that He had control over the physical universe and could change the characteristics of one fluid (water) into another (wine) and could do it instantaneously. This was physically impossible to occur, apart from the creator of the universe transforming the water. On a more human level, we can relate to it. It is similar to an artist who has created an excellent work of art. Let's say it is a painting of a fruit bowl that looks so real that you believe you could take the fruit from the bowl. Suppose the artist doesn't like the way the apple looks like in the bowl and then decides to paint over the apple and paint an orange. It is the artist's creation, and he can make the fruit look however he likes. In the same way, Jesus, as the Creator (see John 1:3), decided to change the water into wine because, like the artist, He can. He revealed to His disciples that He had control over the physical universe and could change it however He wished.

Another insight we gain from the miracle is the quality of the miracle. It is no surprise that the wine Jesus created was excellent. This was noticed by the person in charge of the wedding (the headwaiter), and he made a special point to tell the bridegroom about it. Because of his surprise, the headwaiter vocalized it loud enough that others heard his comments about the wine. Jesus could have changed the water into an ordinary wine, which would still be a miracle, but He chose to turn it into an excellent wine. This is consistent with what we would expect from God in the flesh.

A third insight into this miracle of Jesus was that the miracle was not merely a "magic trick" to awe the crowd. This miracle served others to meet a need. In this case, turning the water into wine served the families of the bride and groom. Imagine the embarrassment they might have experienced before their guests if they had run out of wine. Jesus not only met that need, He did it in a spectacular way by providing, my guess, the best wine they had ever tasted. Many people benefited physically by His miracle and a few benefited spiritually by it.

This miracle introduces us to how Jesus performed miracles. The miracles were amazing and complete. In this case, ALL the water in the stone jars was turned to wine and no trickery was involved. These characteristics will become more evident when Jesus begins His healing ministry. When Jesus healed, the healing was amazing because it was contrary to what they were used to, and the healing completely restored the person from their physical malady. For example, when Jesus healed a blind person, their sight was restored to 20/20 vision. To be silly, they did not have to wear glasses when healed. Just to restore a blind person's sight would have been spectacular, but when Jesus healed, it was complete.

Outcomes from the Miracle

What was the outcome of this miracle? In verse 11, it states He, "…manifested His glory", that is, He showed them a glimpse of who He really is. In seeing this small display of His glory, the disciples' response was they, "…believed in Him". Jesus did not overwhelm the disciples with this miracle, but introduced them to who He is. He confirmed to them that He was the Messiah and more than just a human being. One thing to recognize when we talk about believing, is that belief does not mean we now have a complete understanding. Typically, we start with an immature, yet sincere belief that grows as we gain understanding. My own growth in Christ from when I first believed is a testimony to that. You also see it as you read through any of the Gospel accounts. The disciples' understanding of who the Messiah is, grows as they spend time with Him. There are "bumps in the road" of their faith as they adjust their thinking from what they had been taught about the Messiah versus what Jesus reveals and teaches them.

Even though their faith in Jesus was in the early stages, this does not mean their commitment to Jesus was tentative or conditional. As we discussed in chapter two, they believed in (*eis*) Him. In other words, they were totally committed to Him. They had not spent much time with Jesus, yet, He already had a profound impact on their lives. These five men were already traveling with Jesus in the early stages of His ministry. That is commitment without having a complete understanding of who He is.

John's Purpose Statement in the Light of this Miracle

In the light of John's purpose statement, what was the reason John included this miracle in his account of Jesus's life? John didn't tell us why, but we see the miracle had its intended impact--"His disciples believed in Him." In the latter half of chapter one of the book of John, we see Jesus gathering His first group of disciples--Andrew, Peter, Philip, Nathanael and John. John was likely the unnamed disciple in verses 35-40. These men followed Jesus based upon affirmations on their part that He was the Messiah. In fact, Jesus sees Nathanael in the process of believing when He says in verse 50, "Because I said to you that I saw you under the fig tree, do you believe? You will see greater things than these." In chapter two, the disciples take the next step, as a result of the miracle, and "believe in Him." In other words, Jesus authenticated His credentials as the Messiah, and they placed their trust in Him.

Jesus' life was not merely one of claims. In fact, anyone can make claims about themselves. Jesus took the next step and demonstrated His claims were true by "manifesting His glory" through signs and miracles. We can make the mistake of acknowledging Jesus as merely a historical figure and view His existence intellectually. Just like the disciples, we have to recognize Jesus as more than a person in history. He made claims about Himself that were confirmed by His miracles, and the first confirmation was turning water into wine. I trust our faith is the same as the disciples, with a growing commitment based upon the person and work of Jesus Christ.

Lessons for us from this miracle

Perhaps the most profound lesson from this first miracle is that Jesus meets us where we are spiritually. Jesus met

His disciples where they were in their faith journey and did not overwhelm them with His first miracle. Did it work? Yes! As seen earlier, the disciples believed as a result of this first sign.

In the same way, Jesus meets us where we are, understanding what we need in order to grow in our faith in Him. For some, He may show Himself in a profound way and for others, in a more subtle fashion. In my own faith journey, my first encounter with the Savior was in a dorm room at college with a friend sharing the good news of Christ with me. I remember distinctly thinking to myself, "I want this. I need this." It was God meeting me where I was at in a subtle, but profound way. For others, they meet Christ in a spectacular way. Because of their unique life journey, Jesus "…manifests His glory" in such a way that He is clearly seen. This is the lesson for all of us; Jesus knows each of us intimately and responds to our needs as individuals.

There is also a lesson to be learned from the interaction that Mary had with Jesus that led to this first sign. Mary spoke with confidence that this was the time Jesus should reveal Himself. She knew that Jesus was not going to pull out a talent of gold and tell the servants to go and buy as much wine as they could. She recognized that Jesus would resolve this problem in a supernatural way. Even though Mary had a face-to-face conversation with Jesus, there is a lesson here for us about prayer. Prayer is communication with God. It is bringing our worship, praise, thanksgivings, confessions and supplications to Him. We saw Mary making her supplication to Jesus about the issue of wine without knowing how He would take care of it. But… she talked to Jesus with confidence that He would address this problem. She acted upon her confidence (faith) in Him by preparing the servants to respond to His instruction. In other words, she knew Jesus was going to take care of her request.

We, too, can have a similar confidence in our prayer life as we grow in our relationship with Christ. As mentioned earlier, Mary had a unique relationship with Jesus. She delivered Him into the world and experienced all of the signs and wonders associated with her pregnancy and delivery. She also spent thirty years experiencing life with Him, as she raised the perfect, sinless Son of God. We have a similar privilege of having a unique relationship with the risen Son of God which becomes closer over time as we grow in our relationship with Him. Like Mary, we can become more confident in our prayer life through this growth process.

Finally, the context Jesus chose to perform His first miracle was at a wedding. There were lots of other situations Jesus could have chosen, but there was intentionality in choosing a wedding. He not only wanted to show His disciples that He was the Messiah through turning of the water into wine, but also to affirm marriage through His contribution to the event. Marriage was something that God had created with the first man and woman and now Jesus is subtly saying that marriage is still important and viewed with God's favor and blessing. We see an overt expression of Jesus's view of marriage later in the New Testament (Eph. 5) when Paul uses the imagery of marriage to explain the relationship of Christ (the groom) and the church (the bride). Marriage was sacred when God instituted it in Gen. 2. It was sacred when Jesus affirmed it at the wedding in Cana and it is still sacred today. Let us not allow the culture to dilute this foundational institution which God has created. As an aside, I imagine this was a memorable wedding for the bride and groom at Cana as they were able to piece together what happened behind the scenes.

Jesus's first sign at Cana, as recorded by John, accomplished its intended purpose. The disciples of Jesus believed, as He revealed a glimpse of His glory through turning the water into wine. Jesus had told Nathanael in the previous chapter (1:50), "Because I said to you that I saw you under the fig tree, do you believe? You will see greater things than these." There were many "greater things" the disciples would see in the ministry of Jesus, but at the wedding in Cana, they were introduced to the first sign. Jesus, the Messiah, was in control of the physical universe and could change it however He wished.

As we ponder this sign, we should recognize that Jesus is still in control of the universe and can do whatever He wishes today. He does not have to do miracles today to show Himself as the Son of God, as He did during His time on earth. We have the Word of God which is a record of these miracles. We can be one of those people who Jesus described as, "Blessed *are* they who did not see, and *yet* believed" (Jn. 20:29).

Closing thought

There is much more that could be said about the first sign performed by Jesus, but it would fall outside the scope of this book. There is one insight that I will include here at the end of the chapter because it provides a little more explanation of what was said earlier.

One of the details that John noted concerning the waterpots was their function. The pots held water for the Jewish custom of purification. Murray Harris provides an insight juxtaposing the wine with the water. Harris notes, "The choice wine of the Gospel, kept "until now," has replaced the water of Jewish customs and institutions. This supersession of Judaism by the new revelation of Christ is a recurrent Johannine theme; Jesus has inaugurated the New Order"[1]. The Gospel of John is a book of transition from the old covenant (the Law) to the new covenant (saved through grace by the finished work of Christ on the cross). Jesus is preparing the Jews for this transition by His teachings and His works. Murray is pointing out a subtle sign of this old being replaced with the ceremonial water being replaced with the new wine.

This theme of "new wine" is also seen in the gospel of Matthew, when Jesus said, "…they put new wine into fresh wineskins…" (9:17). In this context, Jesus is saying that the old wineskins (the Law) are not able to hold the new wine without bursting. Therefore, new wineskins are needed to maintain the new wine. We are living in the new covenant age and experiencing the blessing of the new wine in Christ. The Law has accomplished its purpose in showing us how sinful we are. The old wineskins cannot hold what God has given us in Christ Jesus, because it is much greater than the Law.

---

[1] Murray Harris, John in *Exegetical Guide to the Greek New Testament* (Nashville: B&H Publishing, 2015), p. 60.

Chapter 4

MIRACLE #2 IN THE BOOK OF JOHN
HEALING THE ROYAL OFFICIAL'S SON

One activity that grabs our attention are acts of prestidigitation. This is not a common word in our vocabulary, but it means sleight of hand. In other words, we are talking about illusions, magic or trickery with the intent of deceiving the viewer of the trick. That is why we love magic shows. We love to be tricked by the magician even though we know it isn't real and we don't know how they are able to deceive us. The goal of the magician is to take the focus off of him so he can exercise a sleight of hand. On the other hand, the audience is focused on the trick itself and not on the magician. After all, that is why we like to watch magic shows. It is because of the illusions.

In the time that Jesus walked the earth, there were magicians who performed tricks, but with the intent of deceiving their audience into thinking that they had special powers. Then, as today, the audience was taken in by the tricks. When Jesus began performing miracles, starting with turning the water into wine, most of the people who did not know Jesus were enamored with the miracles and not the person who performed the miracle. This is one of the important themes seen in this second miracle highlighted in the Gospel of John--focusing on the person of Jesus versus focusing on the miracles of Jesus.

The miracle described at the end of John 4 is Jesus healing the son of a royal official. Like the miracle of turning water into wine, this miracle is recorded only in John. The setting for this miracle is in Cana, like the previous miracle, but this miracle took place over a year later in Jesus's ministry. Jesus had traveled to Jerusalem for the festival of Passover, met with Nicodemus at night during His time in Jerusalem (John 3), and met with the Samaritan woman on his return trip to Galilee after ministering in Judea (John 4). We know from John 2:23, that during His time at the Passover feast, "...many believed in His name, observing His signs [miracles] which He was doing." We can also surmise that He performed miracles during His ministry in Judea (John 4:1-3). Jesus was developing a reputation that was spreading among the Jews in Judea, Galilee and beyond. This is the context for Jesus's second miracle in Cana.

There are a couple of elements in this miracle story that make it clear why John chose it to support his purpose statement in chapter 20. The key element of this story is the faith of the royal official. This story has three distinct sections to it which show the faith journey that this royal official goes through. He first believes in what Jesus can do, then he believes in what Jesus says and finally he believes in who Jesus is. We will look at how each step of his faith journey manifests itself in this person's life.

Before we delve into the story, let's consider who the "royal official" is. The text gives it away. John describes him as an official who works for royalty. Because he lives in Capernaum, he is within the realm of Herod Antipas, who was a son of Herod the Great and he likely served the king in some capacity. This would indicate that this official was a person with some authority and prestige within his community. He had the financial means to have servants, as highlighted later in the story. Finally, John implies that this official was Jewish since he lived in a predominately Jewish community. John did not see the need to specifically tell us that the official was Jewish. That's all we know about him, and that was all that John determined we needed to know.

Belief in what Jesus can do (vs. 46-49)

This is where the story begins for this royal official. Jesus had returned to Galilee after attending the Passover in Jerusalem. Jesus and His disciples were delayed a couple days in their return trip to Galilee because of a side trip through Samaria where "…many more believed because of His Word…" (vs. 41). This was due to the encounter Jesus had with the Samaritan woman and the recognition by her and many other Samaritans that Jesus was the Messiah.

While in Jerusalem, Jesus was performing signs and miracles which created a reputation of Jesus that spread among the Jews. This reputation spread into Galilee by those who had attended the Passover feast and witnessed the works and teaching of Jesus. The royal official in this story, hearing of the miracles performed by Jesus, was motivated to see Jesus when he found out that Jesus was in Cana. The royal official was from Capernaum and travelled to Cana to plead with Jesus concerning his sick son who was on the verge of death. The distance from Capernaum to Cana is 17-18 miles, as the crow flies, but the distance is much further to travel by land because of the terrain and the elevation change between the two towns (1,700 ft.). This would be a hard one-day trip if he travelled by horse. The official made the commitment to see Jesus because he thought Jesus could heal his son.

This was the first evidence of belief on the part of the official. His faith was incited by all of the stories he had heard about Jesus' healing people and the possibility that Jesus could heal his sick son. In other words, the official's faith was focused on what Jesus could do, trusting in the testimonies of others. His faith in the healing power of Jesus was demonstrated by his commitment to travel to Cana and plead his case to Jesus in person.

As you would expect, when the royal official found Jesus in Cana, he made his request. He wanted Jesus to travel with him back to Capernaum in order to heal his son. You hear the desperation in the official's request for Jesus to heal his son because he is close to death (vs. 47). Jesus's response to him provides an insight into a concern that Jesus had about performing signs and wonders (vs. 48). His concern was that those who witness His miracles would have their faith based upon seeing the miracle not on the person who performed the miracle. Jesus uses strong language here when He says they will *never* believe.

Initially, Jesus's statement seems to contradict John's purpose statement when he said, "…these [signs] have been written so that you may believe…" (20:31). John goes on to clarify the kind of faith these signs should produce, "…believe that Jesus is the Christ, the Son of God." In other words, the focus of Jesus's miracles is to lead the individual to believe in who Jesus is, not in the benefits derived from the miracle. In the case of the royal official, Jesus is saying to him that his faith should not culminate with only seeing a miracle occur in his son's life, but should lead him to believing in the person of Christ.

A second insight we see from Jesus's response to the official, which might not be evident in our English translations, is that He is using the plural "you" not the singular "you". In Southern English, Jesus said, "Unless ya'll see signs and wonders, ya'll will never believe." In other words, He is not speaking to the official as an individual, but he is making a general statement that people will tend to rely upon being eyewitnesses to signs and wonders as the basis for believing. I stated at the beginning of this chapter that seeing is believing, but Jesus is saying that this is not necessarily the case when we talk about genuine faith in Christ. We will see this superficial faith show up again when we look at the miracle of the feeding of the five thousand.

Jesus is testing the genuineness of the official's faith by making this statement about witnessing signs and belief, but the official is undeterred. He responds to Jesus by demanding that Jesus come before his little child dies. This demand by the official is in the imperative tense, which shows the desperation of this man. The official is still of the mindset that Jesus must perform the healing in person. The official makes an adjustment in his second demand by not calling him his son, but making a sympathetic appeal to Jesus by calling him his young child. He also appealed to Jesus by calling Him "Lord." This does not imply that the official now understands that Jesus is the Son of God, but he does recognize that Jesus is a person with the authority to perform miracles, specifically, the authority to heal his young child.

Belief in what Jesus says (vs. 50-52)

The second phase of the royal official's faith journey was his response when Jesus commanded him to go home because his son was healed. In verse 50 it says, "The man **believed** the word that Jesus spoke to him and started off." Unlike the disciples in the first miracle, who believed after witnessing the miracle, this man believed without witnessing the miracle. He left for home, expecting to see his son healed. We see no further dialogue between Jesus and the official. We only see prompt obedience.

Can you imagine what he was thinking about during that 18+ mile and multiple hour trip home? We learn from the text (vs. 52) this was an overnight trip and he probably spent the night at some sort of lodging which made the trip even longer. It was not safe to travel at night due to road bandits. Fortunately, he did not have to wait until he got home to find out how his son was doing. His servants met him on the road and shared the fantastic news that his son was well. In other words, his faith strengthened through their testimony. He confirmed that Jesus was the agent for healing his son by establishing the time when the healing took place. It happened the day before at 1pm, the very time Jesus told him to go because his son lives. The precise time when the healing took place put this miracle outside of the realm of being coincidence and the official recognized this.

The official recognized Jesus' authority to heal, and his faith in Jesus moved from believing in what Jesus could do in performing miracles to believing in the power of Jesus' words to perform miracles. Jesus did not have to be present to exert His authority. He could merely speak, and miracles would happen.

Belief in who Jesus is (vs. 53)

In verse 53, we see the final phase of the royal official's faith journey. He now believes that Jesus is the Christ, the

Son of God. The trigger for this phase of belief was knowing that the hour Jesus said his son lives was the very hour the fever left his son's body and he was healed. What I find amazing is that the official and his household both noted the hour when these events took place.

The text says that the official's whole household believed along with him. By John noting the "whole" household indicated that not only his family believed, but also his servants. The official experienced one aspect of the miracle by being present when Jesus said his son lives. The household experienced the other aspect of the miracle by seeing this child healed of his fever. When both perspectives of the story came together, the whole household drew the same conclusion and believed. We don't want to forget the influence of the official, as head of the household, when he believed. The household's faith was not merely based upon the experience of the official, but also upon what they all experienced.

Summary of the official's faith journey

As we saw above, there were three phases of the royal official's faith journey. The first phase was believing what Jesus could do. The official was looking at Jesus from the perspective that He could help his son get well. In other words, Jesus was an instrument to accomplish what he wanted done--to see his son, who was at death's door, be healed.

The second phase of his faith journey was that the official believed the words Jesus spoke. Jesus spoke with authority and he believed what Jesus said was true. He demonstrated his belief by acting in obedience and heading home to see his healed son.

The final phase of this journey was believing in who Jesus is, the Messiah. Everything came together at this point. What Jesus said came true. The official thought Jesus could do it, Jesus said He did it and the official saw that Jesus had done it.

It was likely when the royal official was hearing the stories of Jesus's miracles, he was also hearing the discussions about whether Jesus was a prophet, or Elijah or the Messiah Himself. The official had the chance to personally see Jesus demonstrate that He was in fact the Messiah when everything came together. This became the final and complete stage of his faith in Jesus as the Messiah.

John's Purpose Statement in Light of this Miracle

How does this miracle fit into John's purpose statement? We gain an insight into this from Jesus Himself. In verse 48, Jesus says to the official, "Unless you *people* see signs and wonders, you *simply* will not believe." Jesus was saying that most of those following Him had a faith based upon what Jesus did, not who He was. In other words, they had a sight-based faith. The royal official was different. He had a **faith-based faith** and demonstrated it by his response to Jesus's words, "Go, your son lives." He believed in what Jesus said and responded in faith to what Jesus commanded without seeing the results until the next day. When he did see the results of what Jesus said, his faith was properly focused on who Jesus is as Messiah, the Son of God.

John wrote this account 50-60 years after this miracle occurred. His audience could not have a sight-based faith in Jesus because He was already in heaven; there were very few people alive who could testify of their experience with Jesus when He walked the earth. We are a part of that same audience who, like the royal official, have a **faith-based faith** that will be realized sometime in the future when we see our Savior in person. This miracle account encourages us to have the same faith as the royal official--a faith based upon who Jesus is and His teachings and works which are recorded in the gospel accounts. This means we believe in the person and work of Jesus on the cross and we commit our lives in accordance with that belief in Him. Jumping ahead in the book of John, Jesus said to his disciple, Thomas, when He revealed Himself to him, "Because you have seen me, have you believed? Blessed are they who did not see, and yet believed" (John 20:29). Jesus is referring to us and we have the words of the book of John to help us in our belief.

Another element of this miracle, that pointed to Jesus as the Son of God, was the unique circumstances of this miracle. Typically, Jesus was present wherever He performed a miracle. In this instance, the sick boy was 18-20 miles away and Jesus merely said, "...your son lives" and the boy was healed. It did not require Jesus to be at the location where the miracle occurred. This harkens back to Genesis one when God merely spoke to bring the creation into existence. For example, "Then God said, "Let the waters below the heavens be gathered into one place, and let the dry land appear; and it was so" (Gen. 1:9). The Genesis one account reinforces what John says about Jesus in chapter one of the Gospel of John, "All things came into being through Him and apart from Him nothing came into being that has come into being" (vs. 3). His authority over the creation is not confined to where He is physically present, but He can speak His will and it happens. Jesus was not a magician, but the creator of the universe.

Lessons for us from this miracle

Like the royal official, our belief should be built on faith, and not on signs and miracles. This means we should place our trust in Jesus even if we don't see any miracles occur in our life. I would venture to guess that most of us reading these words did not place our faith in Christ as a result of a miracle, yet God met us where we were in order for us to hear and respond to the Gospel message. There are stories of individuals, predominantly in Muslim majority countries, that experienced dreams of Jesus appearing to them and these experiences led them to Christ. Whatever way God chooses to meet us, it always comes down to faith in Jesus Christ that leads us to salvation.

On the other hand, we do see God at work by His perfect timing. Suppose Jesus told the official at 5 pm that his son lives and the fever had actually left his son at 1 pm. How would the official react to this or anyone else who heard the story? They would rejoice over the boy's recovery, but would question whether Jesus actually performed the miracle. The expectation is that if Jesus performed the miracle, perfect timing would be a part of the miracle. The same thing applies to us when we see God's hand at work. The timing of events coming together is often the most significant factor in recognizing God's hand at work. I would say that every follower of Christ has a story they can share where they saw events come together in such a way that they recognized God's hand at work.

Even though we don't have Jesus speaking to us face-to-face, He is still speaking to us in His Word, the Bible. The words spoken by Him in the Scriptures are just as powerful as if He had spoken them to us in person. One of the advantages we have over those who heard the words of Jesus spoken in person, is that we have His words written down. We don't have to rely upon our memories to recall what Jesus said and perhaps forget some of those words. This is why we have the written Word of God to read and reference the words of Jesus whenever we want. As we learned from the royal official, there is more than just hearing the words of Jesus. We must obey those words He has spoken to us.

In verse 54 of this chapter of John, he tells us that this was the second sign performed by Jesus in Cana and both of these signs were highlighted by John. Hendriksen describes the nature of these signs, saying, "In both the Lord had manifested his glory. First, by turning the water into wine, he had indicated his absolute control over the physical universe. And now, by means of this second sign, he has shown that distance presents no real obstacle to the manifestation of his power and love"[1]. With both signs, the result was the same. The disciples believed and the royal official and his family also believed when Jesus revealed Himself as the Son of God.

---

[1] William Henriksen, John in *New Testament Commentary* (Grand Rapids: Baker Academic, 1953), p. 184

Chapter 5

MIRACLE #3 IN THE BOOK OF JOHN
THE HEALING AT THE POOL OF BETHESDA

Many of you have probably heard of the inkblot test that some psychologists administer to their patients. Technically, it is called the Rorschach Test, named after the psychologist who developed this evaluation tool. The test is comprised of symmetrical inkblots the patient views and then describes what they see. What the patient sees will then help the psychologist determine what is going on inside the patient. Their mental state will influence how they see the inkblots. The Rorschach Test aside, our thinking can influence how we interpret what we see. Depending upon the experiences and biases each person has, they can see the same thing, but draw different conclusions This will become evident as we examine the third miracle recorded by John and see the different reactions to this miracle.

This third miracle is recorded in verses 2-9 of chapter five. To gain insights into the miracle itself and the repercussions of this miracle with the Jews, we will also discuss verses 10-17. Remember, we are looking at each of the miracles in the book of John from the perspective of John's purpose statement. In a nutshell, we are examining how each of the miracles leads us to believing who Jesus is and, as a result of that belief, have eternal life.

This third miracle, like the first two, is only recorded in the Gospel of John. The setting for this miracle is in Jerusalem during *a feast*. The text does not tell us which feast it is, but it is not likely the Feast of Passover because it was previously mentioned in the context of the healing of the royal official's son. Also, the beginning of chapter five says, "After these things…" pointing back to the second miracle. The feast mentioned here is likely one of the other two feasts that the Jews were required to attend in Jerusalem (Pentecost or Feast of the Booths). Whereas, knowing the name of the feast is not essential to John's story, we do know there were a lot of people in Jerusalem attending this feast.

The setting for this miracle

John directs us to the focal location of Jesus's next miracle. John says, "…there is in Jerusalem by the Sheep *Gate* a pool, which is called in Hebrew, Bethesda, having five porticoes" (vs. 2). During His visit in Jerusalem, Jesus went to this pool, located in the northeast section of Jerusalem, north of the temple. There were actually two pools. There is a large pool and a small one, separated by a wall, and connected by a canal between them. These pools are larger than your typical swimming pool or even an Olympic-sized swimming pool. The combined size of the two pools are 131 yards long and 55 yards wide. Also, the depth of the pools are approximately 45 ft. To give you some perspective on the size of the pools, an NFL football field is 120 yards long and 53 yards wide. The pools were surrounded by covered porches (*five porticoes*) which provided protection to those visiting the pool. The two pools were built at separate times in Israel's history. The larger pool was built sometime after the building of the first temple by Solomon and was used as a water reservoir, perhaps for the temple. Later, in the 200s B.C., a second pool was built and connected to the first by a canal, to allow water to flow from the large pool to the small one. The archaeological evidence shows that the second pool was used as a public *mikveh*, a place for Jewish pilgrims to ritually purify themselves before entering the temple.[1] There was a lot of activity around the Pool of Bethesda, particularly during the feasts.

Included with the crowds of pilgrims purifying themselves in the *mikveh* was a variety of people lying around the pool. John describes these people as, "…sick, blind, lame and with withered…" (vs. 2). The *withered* is talking about individuals with withered limbs or bodies. These people were not there to become ritually clean, because they were disqualified from entering the temple due to their maladies. They were at the pool with the hope of being healed. This was a popular place for these individuals because of the hope it provided. As we saw described above, the area around the pool was large enough to hold a *multitude* of people with the same hope and desire in mind. A story had been popularly circulated that the water in the pool had healing power when the water was stirred up (see verse 7). This is what drew all of these people to the pool.

This story about the healing power of the water, which is included in most translations of the Gospel of John, is about an angel who would periodically stir the water. The first infirmed person to step into the pool after the water was stirred would be healed of their affliction. You probably noticed in your Bible that the last part of verse two and all of verse three is placed in brackets and/or a note is included saying that the early manuscripts of John did not contain this text. Most scholars believe the last part of verse three and all of verse four were a later insertion and not a part of the original manuscript of John. There is a variety of reasons for this conclusion, which I will not delve into, but it appears a later scribe felt the need to include this in the text to provide background to the story.[2] This particular story was in circulation in the early church, but it was not necessarily the same story that was disseminated during the time this event took place.

In all the chaos, with the crowds attempting to enter the *mikveh* and people lying around the pool with the hope of being healed, Jesus initiates a conversation with a sick man who did not know Jesus. We do not know what kind of infirmity the man had, but it was debilitating enough to prevent him from entering the pool on his own, if and when the waters stirred. We read from the account that Jesus immediately heals this man and being back to full health, he is able to walk again. There are four insights we will look at that give us a better understanding of this miracle.

Four insights from this miracle

First, the man did not approach or call out to Jesus to be healed. His healing was not because of his belief that Jesus could restore him to full health. He did not even know Jesus. When Jesus asked the man if he wanted to be made well, he could only think about someone helping him enter the pool first after the waters were stirred. He had no idea of what was going to happen until it occurred. Jesus simply said, "Pick up your pallet and walk." The man was immediately made well because Jesus chose to heal him, apart from anything the man said, did, or believed. In other words, Jesus, within the character and eternal will of God, can do whatever He wants, whenever He wants, to whomever He wants. Jesus exercised this authority with the sick man.

Out of all the people lying around the Pool of Bethesda, the question arises as to why Jesus chose this person to be healed. The easy answer is because it was God's will. A more complete answer is that God was accomplishing His purposes for him and us in healing this man. This was not a random decision on Jesus' part, like casting lots to make the decision or because the man smiled when Jesus saw him. We don't know all of the reasons Jesus chose to heal this man, but we do know that Jesus knew the man outwardly and He knew him inwardly. Jesus knew who he was, his background, and why he was lying by the pool. Jesus chose this infirmed man to show him and us the authority He has over sickness and sin.

Secondly, after Jesus disappears in the crowd after healing the man (verse 13), the man's first response is to go to the temple. This is where Jesus later finds him. After thirty-eight years of being disqualified from entering the temple, he is now, physically, a whole man and can participate in temple activities. The Pool of Bethesda was about 200 yards north of the temple area; therefore, it was easy for him to go there, especially with those strong legs that had just been restored. The text does not explain why he went to the temple, but it makes sense that he wanted to tell the religious leaders that he was healed of his infirmity. What happened is that the Jews questioned him because he was violating the Sabbath. They saw him walking with a mat under his arm, breaking rabbinic law. We will delve into this Sabbath controversy later on.

Thirdly, Jesus gives us an insight into why the man was ill. To find this out, we have to jump to verse 14. When Jesus found him later at the temple, He said to him, "Behold, you have become well; do not sin anymore, so that nothing worse happens to you." Jesus is clearly implying that this unnamed man, who had been ill for thirty-eight years, was infirmed because of a sin or sins in his life. It was a popular theological belief among the Jews in the time of Jesus that infirmities were directly related to sin. In other words, the automatic conclusion was drawn that a person was sick because of some sin in their life. In this particular case, there was a direct relationship between the man's sin and the illness he had experienced because Jesus pointed it out. The man probably could recall the sin(s) he had committed thirty-eight years ago that led to this disabling illness. As we read through the New Testament, we do see that sin does have physical consequences, including illness. One example is found in 1 Corinthians 11 concerning those believers who take the Lord's Supper in an unworthy manner. Paul says to them that judgment will come upon them and, "For this reason many among you are weak and sick, and a number sleep [died]" (vs. 30). Sin can have a direct, physical cause and effect relationship, or it can bring judgment from God upon them, as Paul described in 1 Corinthians 11. We don't know which of these effects the infirmed man experienced, but you get the sense, by the warning Jesus gives him, that the latter had come upon him. (We will see later in the Gospel of John, when Jesus heals the man who was blind from birth, that there is a third reason for having infirmities.)

We find that Jesus does give this man a second chance by commanding him not to sin anymore. Jesus demonstrated that He could and did counteract the effects of this man's sin by restoring him and Jesus is warning him not to let it happen again. It needs to be clarified that Jesus is not saying, "If you sin one more time, then it is going to be bad for you." He is saying that if the man continues in the sin he had committed before, then the consequences are going to be even worse. When Jesus speaks of a worse condition for this man, He may be referring to his future spiritual state. In other words, Jesus is giving him a serious warning that impacts eternity.

The last insight we see is that Jesus performed this miracle on the Sabbath. This raised the ire of the Jews because He commanded the man whom He had just healed to, "Pick up your pallet and walk." The Jews were not focused on the miracle, nor were they rejoicing to see a man who had been ill for thirty-eight years be made whole, but they were offended, seeing their definition of the Sabbath law being violated. Even though the Old Testament gives a general description of a Sabbath rest, the rabbis defined what rest from labor meant with thirty-nine primary categories of labor. The last category of labor mentioned in the Mishnah was, "...one who carries out an object from domain to domain" (*Shabbat*, vii, 2)[3]. Clearly, the healed man was guilty of violating the Sabbath, according to the Jews. As you read the gospel accounts, "properly" observing the Sabbath created a huge conflict between the Jews and Jesus. The main point Jesus is making here, as well as elsewhere, is that He is the Lord over the Sabbath because He is the Son of Man. He is the one who instituted the Sabbath and He is the one who best understands how it should be observed. Jesus was not only making claims about Himself and His relationship with the Father (see verse 17), He substantiated those claims by the signs and miracles He performed.

It is interesting to see the interaction between the healed man and the Jews when discussing this issue. The point, the healed man was making during his interactions with the Jews, was that Jesus made me well. In contrast, the Jews were focused on who told you to pick up your mat and violate the Sabbath. We do not have clear evidence from the text whether the man believed in Jesus as the Messiah, but he clearly recognized that Jesus had made him physically whole after thirty-eight years of being sick.

John's Purpose Statement in Light of this Miracle

As per John's purpose statement, Jesus revealed more about who He was through this miracle. Jesus demonstrated His power (lordship) over sickness and His lordship over God's Law. Though it was not generally understood among the crowds that followed Jesus, the religious leaders clearly understood Jesus's claims. They understood that Jesus, "...was calling God His own Father, making Himself equal with God" (verse 18). The religious leaders were blind to the fact that Jesus's words were backed up by the works He performed. The key was believing in Jesus as *the Messiah*, *the Son of God*, and these leaders refused to believe, even though they heard His words and witnessed the signs and miracles He performed.

There were two reasons the religious leaders responded so negatively to Jesus's works and message, to the point that they initiated a plot to kill him. The first reason was that the Jews had created their picture of the Messiah with requirements for who the Messiah is, how he is to act and what he would do for the Jewish people. Jesus was not meeting those requirements, particularly in the context of this story, because He prioritized healing an infirmed man over "keeping" the Sabbath.

The second reason the religious leaders responded negatively to Jesus was that they wanted to maintain their power. Jesus threatened that power because of His growing popularity with the people. It was all about themselves. Fortunately, this did not characterize all of the religious leaders. Some were earnestly looking for the Messiah and came to believe in Jesus. One of those leaders, who was introduced to us by John in chapter three, was "…a man of the Pharisees, named Nicodemus, a ruler of the Jews…" (vs. 1).

Even though we did not see many religious leaders believe in Jesus, John was clear in John 20:31, when he said, "…these things were written so that you **may [might]** believe…". The miracle that Jesus performed upon the infirmed man showed us that Jesus is the Christ, but it did not mean that everyone who saw the miracle or the outcome of the miracle believed in Him. In other words, no guarantee exists that everyone who witnesses or reads about Jesus will accept. The religious leaders clearly demonstrated this by their response to Jesus. We know it takes a work of the Holy Spirit to open our blind eyes to see the truth that Jesus is the Messiah, the Son of God.

Lessons for us from this miracle

This event, which occurred 2,000 years ago, has relevance for us today. The reason for this relevance is because the sin nature of humanity has not changed and the God of the universe has not changed either. The first takeaway for us from this story is the response of the parties involved in this miracle. Nowhere in this story does the word, *believe,* show up. Even with the healed man, we do not know if he recognized who Jesus really was and believed in Him. After he told the Jews that Jesus healed him, he leaves the story without further comment.

What a contrast we see with this story compared to the previous story of the royal official. The official did not see the miracle take place, but saw the result of it and he believed and all his household also believed. It was very clear they understood who Jesus was and responded in faith. The religious leaders saw the results of what Jesus had done to the infirmed man and they responded with hate.

Even today, contrasts are going to be seen when individuals have an encounter with Jesus and the good news of the gospel. There will be those who embrace the gospel and believe in Jesus. There will be those who are indifferent to the gospel and walk away. Finally, there will be those who actively oppose the gospel and will express their opposition through words or deeds.

Secondly, this event is relevant today because our view of God can impact our understanding of Him. Most people today would say they are not caught up in the legalism like the Jews were in this story, which distorted their image of the Messiah. It can be said that most people have a view of God in which God is "created in their own image" rather than what the Scriptures tell us. For example, many people have a difficult time seeing God as a loving, heavenly Father, because of the negative encounters they experienced with their own earthly father growing up. If they were abused by an alcoholic father growing up, it will be difficult for them to see God as being a loving, caring father. Their experiences will cause them to have a bias against God, therefore, preventing them from seeing God as He has shown Himself in the Bible.

We are privileged to have the Bible to read and from which we gain a correct understanding of who God is. This is one of the reasons God gave us His written Word. He wants to show Himself to us as He really is and not through the lenses of people interpreting who He is. The miracles that John presents to us through his gospel account is a way to paint a true picture of who God is and also who His Son is. Jesus came to this earth to show us the Father.

One of the key points derived from the healing of the infirmed man is the consequences of sin. This man suffered for thirty-eight years because of the destructive nature of sin. Even though we don't know the end of the story for him, we know Jesus gave him a second chance. This event is relevant to us because sin has implications for everyone. We know that sin does not impact every human in the same way as it did with the man in this story, but we do know that sin does affect every human being. Sin alienates us from God, and it began with our first parents, Adam and Eve, when they chose to disobey God. This still plagues us today, because every human being has made that same choice to disobey God over and over. Our fundamental nature is one of being rebellious towards God.

Fortunately, God addressed this sin problem and the eternal consequences of sin through Jesus's coming to this earth and dying on the cross for our sins. We will discuss this event later in our study of the miracles found in John. One thing that is critical to say at this point is that with Jesus' death, burial and resurrection from the dead, He gave us a second chance like He did with the infirmed man. The sick man experienced the physical consequences of his sin reversed by being healed, but we can see the eternal consequences of our sins reversed through believing in Jesus.

---

[1] For more information on the Pool of Bethesda, I would recommend an article in the magazine, *Biblical Archaeology Review*, September/October 2011, called *The Puzzling Pool of Bethesda*, authored by Urban C. von Wahlde. It provides a comprehensive overview of the current understanding of the pool. This article can be found via https://library.biblicalarchaeology.org/article/the-puzzling-pool-of-bethesda/

[2] See Murray Harris, John in *Exegetical Guide to the Greek New Testament* (Nashville: B&H Publishing, 2015), p. 105, for a good summary.

[3] I quoted from the Mishnah as my source for the Sabbath rules observed by the Jews. The Mishnah is a collection of rabbinic customs, practices, and opinions collected around A.D. 200. Most of this collection includes what was practised by the Jews before the temple was destroyed in A.D. 70, which consists of the time Jesus was walking the earth. The Mishnah is a collection of tractates (treatises) that deal with different aspects of the religious life of a Jew. As you might guess, a tractate written called Shabbat addressed the parameters of labor a Jew could do on the Sabbath. It is believed these rules do go back to the time of Christ.

As another side note about the Sabbath rules for labor, the Jews would not have rejoiced over the healing of the infirmed man, even if he had not violated the rule about carrying objects. The rabbis also had rules about caring for someone who was sick or injured on the Sabbath. The general principle they established was, "...all danger to life was to supersede the Sabbath" (Emil Schürer, *A History of the Jewish People in the Time of Jesus Christ*, Div.

2, Vol. ii (Peabody, MA: Hendrickson Publishers, 1890), p. 104). In other words, the infirmed man was not in danger of dying, therefore, Jesus violated the Sabbath by caring (healing) for him.

Chapter 6

Miracle #4 in the Book of John
Feeding the Five Thousand

You have probably seen a nature show where the predator is sneaking up on a group of unsuspecting prey. When the herd is aware of the predator's presence, they all flee together to escape the danger. They act in one accord without thinking about what they are doing. This is called a herd mentality and this mentality applies to human groups also. Merriam-Webster dictionary defines a herd mentality as, "the tendency of the people in a group to think and behave in ways that conform with others in the group rather than as individuals"[1]. In other words, the group drives the behavior, and often without individual introspection. This can have positive and negative results depending upon the behavior of the crowd. How many times have we seen riots on TV with individual participants who have no understanding about why they are rioting? It is driven by the group they are a part of.

This herd mentality will show up with the next miracle we look at in the book of John. We will see this at work with a collective misunderstanding of who Jesus is, because it is driven by wanting their stomachs full.

The fourth miracle that John records in the book of John (chapter 6) is the feeding of the five thousand. This miracle takes a dramatic turn in John's record of miracles because this miracle is not focused on an individual, but on a whole group of people. This miracle is also recorded by all four of the gospel writers which tells us how significant this miracle was with them. This miracle would also be familiar to most of the readers of John since the books of Matthew, Mark and Luke were already in circulation by the time the Gospel of John was released. John did not see repeating this story as a useless repetition, but deemed this miracle important enough to help fulfil his purpose statement in chapter 20. This miracle helps us to see and believe that Jesus is the Christ, the Son of God.

Let's consider some of the details John includes in his description of this miracle, which help us understand Jesus' claims.

Setting the scene

John describes this miracle's scene by describing where Jesus and His disciples travelled. Based upon a composite description by the gospel writers, they travelled by boat to Bethsaida, located in the northeast section of the Sea of Galilee (also called the Sea of Tiberias). Another important detail the synoptic writers (Matthew, Mark and Luke) give us about the location is that it was *desolate*. This means they were near Bethsaida, but were still some distance away from it, as well as other towns and villages in the area. The reason Jesus chose this location was to get away from the crowd. In Mark 6:31, it states, "And He said to them, "Come away by yourselves to a secluded place and rest a while." (For many people were coming and going, and they did not even have time to eat.)" Even though Jesus was the Son of God, He was still human and needed rest from the press of humanity biding for His time.

Despite His efforts to get away from the people to rest, they still found Him and in significant numbers. It is revealed in verse nine that five thousand men were present to see Jesus, and Matthew adds that this five thousand does not include women and children (Mt. 14:21). By approximation, perhaps there were fifteen thousand people or more at this location. John tells us why they were there, "…they saw the signs which He was performing on those who were sick" (vs. 2). The people were drawn by what Jesus could do, not what He taught.

We also know the time of year when this event took place. In verse four, John says, "Now the Passover, the feast of the Jews, was near." Passover always occurred in the spring, and the Feast of the First Fruits was part of the Passover celebration. This Feast of First Fruits celebrated the barley harvest, which was the first harvest of the spring season. John provides another small detail: the area had much grass (vs. 10), consistent with the springtime of year when the land was flourishing from the early rains.

Seeking a human solution for the problem

Jesus prepared the disciples for this miracle rather than merely performing it. He prepared them by allowing them to see that there was no human way this huge crowd of people could be fed with the resources they had on hand.

Matthew, Mark, and Luke highlight that it was evening when the discussion began among the disciples about how the people should be fed. This is important to note, because the first option the disciples suggested to Jesus was to disperse the crowd in order that they might go into the local towns and villages to find food and lodging for the night. On the surface, this sounds like a smart solution until we realize two challenges-- 1) there are approximately fifteen thousand people involved to find food and lodging and 2) the crowd is in a remote location, which, by definition, would mean there are few people living in the area. Even if the crowd was dispersed, the local resources would be quickly overwhelmed by the needs of so many people.

Jesus now reinforces the acuteness of this food problem by telling the disciples, "You give them something to eat" (Mt. 14:16; Mk. 6:37; Lk. 9:13). In the Gospel of John,

John writes that Jesus specifically asks Philip, "Where are we to buy bread that they may eat?" (vs. 5). Jesus is asking Philip to do a cost analysis of the situation. He is asking Philip if the crowd could be fed with the money that is available to buy food. Jesus and the disciples had a money box with funds to be used for expenses while doing ministry. In John 13:29, it says Judas Iscariot was the disciple with the money box. Philip completed his analysis and came back to Jesus to report that "Two hundred denarii worth of bread is not sufficient for them, for everyone to receive a little" (vs. 7). There is not enough money to feed this crowd!

To give you a sense of the money involved, we will compare the value of a denarius in today's dollars. The common understanding of the value of a denarius, in the time of Jesus, was equivalent to one day's wage of a common laborer. If we equate that to a wage of $10.00/hr. or $80.00/day, then two hundred denarii would be worth $16,000. If we divided that $16,000 among fifteen thousand people, each person would get $1.06 worth of food. As Philip said, each person would *receive a little*.

If Philip had determined they had enough money to buy what was needed to feed the crowd, where would they go to get the food? This is the same problem described above with the "dispersal" solution. For example, bread is baked on a daily basis in the morning, based upon the demand for bread for that day. In the evening, it would have been difficult to find a large supply of bread, let alone other food in this *remote* area.

It should be noted here, as is noted in the text, that Jesus already knew the answer to the problem the disciples were working on. He knew there was not a human solution to this problem. As it is stated in verse six, Jesus, "…was saying this *only* to test him, for He Himself knew what he intended to do." He was not trying to frustrate Philip and the other disciples, but was trying to strip them of all human possibilities for feeding this crowd. The word that John used here for test (*peirazo*), has the idea of a test that would lead to a negative result. In other words, Jesus knew they would not pass the test. He wanted them to also realize they could not pass the test by human means.

Finally, Andrew confirms the dire nature of the situation by reporting on how much food is currently available among the people. John also includes two details, which are absent in the other gospel accounts, about the type of food available. First, he tells us the five bread cakes were made of barley. This gives us an insight into the demographics of the crowd. We know they were generally poor because they had no food, and the barley bread they had was "…the cheap, staple food of the poorer classes"[2]. Those in the higher classes ate wheat bread. John also uses a specific word for the two fish, *opsarion*, that was available. The literal meaning of this word for fish combines small and cooked. These fish were probably small, dried fish used in cooking relish. This is what you would expect from a crowd of poorer people who did not have any food with them. It appears the crowd (herd) mentality had stepped in, and the crowd followed Jesus without thinking about their personal needs when they ended up at this remote location.

Providing a divine solution for the problem

Jesus created the circumstances for this miracle to show the disciples that there was nothing humanly possible they could do to feed this crowd of fifteen thousand men, women and children. Dispersing the crowd to buy food, sending the disciples to buy two hundred denarii of food, if available, or distributing the five loaves of bread and two small fish at hand would not work. This was the reason all the questions and investigations were conducted. With the human options exhausted, Jesus took the bread and the fish, blessed the food and then had the disciples distribute the food. We gain insight from Luke about the food distribution when Jesus tells the disciples, "Have them recline to eat in groups of about fifty each" (Lk. 9:15). We see from this instruction that Jesus was organizing the crowd to distribute the food efficiently. It also provided a method to count the number of people in the crowd accurately. They likely only counted the men to make the counting easier.

Jesus clearly showed his disciples and those in the crowd, who could witness it, that by first blessing the food, this was a sign from God. As it is typical with any of the miracles Jesus does, the hungry crowd did not get "just enough" food, but as much as they wanted to be *satisfied*. Again, this confirms the kind of miracles Jesus performs. As we have already seen, He completely heals the sick people and creates first-class wine out of water. Would you expect anything different from the Son of God? As Henricksen notes, "...he does not just create bread, but changes bread into more bread. This was entirely in line with the purpose of his coming to the earth. He had come not to create, but to transform, and... whenever he gives, he gives lavishly."[3]. This reminds us of the grace God has poured out on us, as followers of Christ. Ephesians 1:7-8a says, "In Him we have redemption through His blood, the forgiveness of our trespasses, according to the **riches** of His grace which He **lavished** on us." This is jumping ahead in the story, but it confirms the generosity God has and wants to pour out on us.

The richness of His generosity is further seen in this story with the leftovers. After the whole crowd ate until they were full, Jesus had the disciples pick up the leftover bread. "And so, they gathered them up, and filled twelve baskets with fragments from the five barley loaves, which were left over by those who had eaten" (Jn. 6:13). Jesus did not give them just enough, but more than enough food. We don't know how large these baskets were, but they had to be substantial enough that all of the gospel writers felt this should be included in their narrative.

The reaction to the miracle

Both the disciples and the crowd recognized the miracle which occurred, as evidenced by their full stomachs and the twelve baskets of leftover bread. The crowd responded to this miracle by proclaiming Jesus as "...the Prophet who has come into the world." Perhaps they were associating Jesus and the multiplication of bread with Moses and the manna which the LORD provided in the wilderness. More likely, they were identifying Jesus with Moses and *the Prophet* described in Deut. 18:15, "The LORD your God will raise up for you a prophet like me from among you, from your countrymen, you shall listen to him." It was understood by the Jews that this prophet was the Messiah, who would be a mediator, like Moses, between the LORD and man.

The problem with their identification of Jesus as *the Prophet* is that they had an incomplete picture of the Messiah. The crowd was ready to make Him an earthly king that would benefit them rather than hearing His message of being the Savior of the world. This may explain why John gave us the date marker in verse four that, "…the Passover, the feast of the Jews, was near." Passover is one of the festivals that all Jews are required to attend. Possibly the crowd was going to take Jesus to Jerusalem to coronate Him as King of the Jews. Jesus was not taken in by this because He knew His popularity was based upon what He did, not who He was. In fact, the crowd was a year early in "coronating" Jesus. At Passover the following year, Jesus would make His triumphal entry into Jerusalem.

What a contrast in response we see with this crowd and the response of the Jews in chapter five of John. Both groups had misunderstood who Jesus was based upon their image of the Messiah and they reacted to Him in polar opposite ways. This crowd was ready to crown Him as king and the Jews in Jerusalem were ready to kill Him at the first opportunity. But neither group saw Jesus as He really is and how He presented Himself.

How did Jesus respond to their desire for Him to be king? He "...withdrew again to the mountain by Himself alone" (Jn. 6:15). It was not the right time. Jesus knew exactly when that time would be that He would fulfill His mission, as commissioned by the Father.

John's purpose statement in light of this miracle

The feeding of the five thousand was a considerable departure from the signs and miracles Jesus had been doing. His ministry had focused on healing individuals, and now several thousand people were directly impacted by His miraculous multiplication of food. This miracle further revealed Jesus as the Christ, the Son of God, by showing us His concern for their basic needs, and then meeting those needs. Though it is not stated in John, the accounts of Matthew and Mark talk about Jesus's compassion for the crowd, "...because they were like sheep without a shepherd" (Mk. 6:34).

This miracle revealed how we can misunderstand who Jesus really is when we focus only on the physical. Clearly, this crowd had been taken in by all of His healings (see verse 3), and now they saw that everyone could benefit physically from His ministry. Jesus also saw this, and knowing the heart of the crowd, He withdrew Himself to a quiet place in the mountain.

As we can see, the miracle of feeding the five thousand was recorded by all four gospel writers, with John adding some unique details to the story. We also know why he included this story in light of his purpose statement. Still, the biggest reason for including this miracle is seen later in chapter six, which is only recorded in the John account. The next day, he explained to the crowd, which followed Him from the feeding site, a deeper meaning behind the bread, which was more than just filling their stomachs. The physical feeding aimed to point them to Jesus, the bread of life. He tells them, "…he who comes to Me will not hunger and he who believes in Me will never thirst" (vs. 35). Jesus uses the strongest possible words to say they will *never* hunger and *never* thirst. What a contrast to the momentary satisfaction of being physically filled with bread. It is in Jesus Himself where our belief must lie, for "…everyone who beholds the Son, and believes in Him will have eternal life" (vs. 40).

What do we learn from the feeding of the five thousand? When we have an incomplete picture of who Jesus is, it will lead to wrong conclusions. The crowd was close to genuine belief by correctly assessing that Jesus was *the Prophet*, but they did not see that the bread was pointing them to Jesus, the bread of life. The crowd was deceived by focusing on the physical and missing out on what Jesus had to offer-- the bread of life. We must be on alert and not allow ourselves to be deceived similarly.

Lessons for us from this miracle

The big lesson from this miracle was that Jesus showed the disciples and the crowd that the physical bread pointed to Jesus as the bread of life, and our belief should lie in Him as the bread of life. There are also other practical lessons to be learned from this miracle.

First, we are just like the disciples trying to figure out every human way possible to solve a problem, rather than first looking to God for the answer. We focus on our abilities to solve problems and when we run out of those options, then we finally look to God. Jesus is typically our backup except when we are in a dire situation beyond our control.

Secondly, Jesus does and will take care of our basic needs. We tend to see basic needs, food, housing, and a car, as our responsibility and God takes care of the bigger problems. We fail to recognize that God wants to take care of our basic needs. There is part of the Lord's Prayer that we tend to pray right over, "…Give us this day our daily bread…" (Mt. 6:11). What Jesus is saying with this prayer is that we should rely upon God for our daily needs. That doesn't mean that we should not work, and simply trust Him. After all, the Apostle Paul stated in 2 Thessalonians 3:11, "…if anyone is not willing to work, then he is not to eat, either." This means that we should recognize that God is the one who has given us the job, the skills to do the job, and the health to maintain the job. It **all** comes from Him for us to have our daily bread. In summary, Jesus said, "…your heavenly Father knows that you need all these things. But seek first His kingdom and His righteousness and all these things will be added to you" (Mt. 6:32-33). The priority is to pursue God and He will take care of our needs.

This fourth miracle of Jesus points to something greater than God meeting our basic physical needs. It is pointing to Jesus meeting our basic spiritual needs. If we only focus on our physical needs, then we will miss what Jesus meant when He said He was the bread of life. Our physical bread will only satisfy us for a few hours and then we will hunger for more. When we take the spiritual bread that Jesus has to offer, we will never hunger again because our deepest spiritual needs have been satisfied. Our deepest spiritual need is to have our relationship with God restored and Jesus accomplished this when He died on the cross for our sins. We only have to believe in Him to experience eternal life and enjoy the bread that satisfies us forever.

---

[1] https://www.merriam-webster.com/dictionary/herd mentality Accessed 9/25/24.

[2] Murray Harris, John in *Exegetical Guide to the Greek New Testament* (Nashville: B&H Publishing, 2015), p. 123.

[3] William Hendriksen, John in *New Testament Commentary* (Grand Rapids: Baker Academic, 1953), p. 223.

Chapter 7

MIRACLE #5 IN THE BOOK OF JOHN
WALKING ON WATER

If you own a home and/or a car, you also have insurance for those pieces of property. Insurance is required by law to protect you and others if an accident or damage occurs to your auto or home. One type of damage is included in every insurance policy. It is called "an act of God". This term describes an event not caused by any direct human action. Typically, the term describes a weather event, like a tornado, which has caused property damage. Even though this is a legal term, it acknowledges that God controls the natural events. Those who say "an act of God" may not take it seriously, but we should take it very seriously because it is true, and Jesus demonstrated it in John 6, right after feeding the five thousand.

John continues to demonstrate that "...Jesus is the Christ, the Son of God" with the fifth miracle he describes in the book of John. This miracle is on the heels of the feeding of the five thousand, showing His control over His creation. This makes sense in light of chapter one, when John says in verse 3, "all things came into being through Him [Jesus], and apart from Him nothing came into being that has come into being." In other words, Jesus is the Lord of creation, and the creation bows down to His will. It is very clear in this miracle that Jesus is Lord because He defies the laws of physics.

Setting the scene

This miracle is also recorded in the books of Matthew and Mark, but John leaves out many of the details in the other accounts. Perhaps John felt that a more abbreviated account (6:16-21) would accomplish the goal of his purpose statement in chapter 20, since many of his readers would already be familiar with the story from hearing Matthew and/or Mark. This story is a continuation of the feeding of the five thousand, with Jesus, "...withdrawing to the mountain by Himself alone" (Jn. 6:15). Jesus needed to get alone to spend time with His Father and to get away from the crowd, who wanted to take Him to Jerusalem to coronate Him as king.

Jesus sends His disciples on their way, by boat, to head back to Capernaum, their ministry base. Nothing in the story tells us how Jesus was going to catch up with them, but it appears the disciples were comfortable leaving Him behind. It was now past the evening hours and the disciples were taking off when it was dark (vs. 17). It may seem strange for the disciples to take off when it was dark, but some of them were fishermen and they were used to being on the sea all night to fish (see Jn. 21:3-4).

The miracle of walking on water

One of the things the disciples did not predict when they took off in their boat was the weather conditions. Storms can rise up easily on the Sea of Galilee because of its location, being surrounded by hills. This allows for strong winds to sweep across the water, which makes for dicey conditions. In this case, the strong winds also stirred up the sea, making the conditions even more difficult. One thing the gospel writers did not say about the disciples in the boat was that they were afraid. It appears the fishermen on the boat had experienced conditions like this before and they knew what to do. This is in contrast to a previous experience the disciples had when they were caught in a storm on this same sea. That time, Jesus was with them and He was asleep while the storm was raging (see Mt. 8:24-27; Mk. 4:37-41; Lk. 8:23-25). The storm was severe enough that they were *very much afraid* and they cried out to the sleeping Son of God, "Save us, Lord; we are perishing!" (Mt. 8:25). When Jesus awoke, He rebuked the storm and the sea immediately became calm.

The disciples, in this second recorded encounter with a stormy sea, took evasive action to deal with the storm.

They begin rowing the boat toward their destination. The wind was probably blowing the boat in a direction they did not want to go and they had to rely upon rowing to stay on course. Though not stated in the text, it seems reasonable to assume that they took the sail down in order to keep the wind from controlling the direction of the boat. John says they rowed 25-30 stadia toward their destination. By calculation, they had rowed between 2.87-3.45 miles. With the rough seas, it would have taken quite a bit of effort and quite a bit of time to go this distance.

We know the disciples have been out on the sea for quite a while, based upon Matthew and Mark telling us it was, "...the fourth watch of the night" (Mt.14:25; Mk. 6:48) when something quite unexpected happened. The fourth watch is between 3-6 am, therefore, they had been out on the sea most of the night. The disciples were probably very tired from all they had experienced over the past twenty-four hours. It was at this point that Jesus showed up on the scene. They had last seen Him going up the hill to pray, and now they were experiencing the impossible: Jesus was walking on water and coming toward them! Jesus showed up at the right time. He had not forgotten about them when He was spending time with His Heavenly Father, but knew their situation well. He demonstrated His divine power by the timing of His arrival and His method of travel.

The disciples were not afraid of the storm, but they were afraid when Jesus showed up. Both Matthew and Mark state that the disciples initially thought He was a ghost because this was how they were processing what they were seeing with the wind, the waves and the darkness blurring their vision. The ghost image made more sense to them than the flesh-and-blood Jesus walking on the water. Jesus was not walking on a smooth sea, but a sea stirred up by a strong wind. You can understand the fear the disciples were experiencing.

Jesus understood their fear and commanded them, "...do not be afraid" (vs. 20). This command of authority reassured the disciples that He was in charge and would take care of them. Jesus spoke like a father trying to comfort his children in a difficult situation. Before issuing this command, Jesus identified Himself to the disciples with the statement, "It is I." Literally, what Jesus said to the disciples was, "I AM", or it could be translated, "I am *he*." Both are correct, but the context helps us understand whether Jesus is merely identifying Himself to the disciples or using God's divine name. God used this name when He identified Himself to Moses in the burning bush in Exodus 3:13-14. Matthew, Mark, and John recorded the same greeting Jesus had given the disciples. The strongest clue that Jesus was identifying Himself with the divine name is found in Matthew's account of the event. In Matthew 14:32-33, he states, "And when they [Peter and Jesus] got into the boat, the wind stopped. And those who were in the boat worshipped Him, saying, "You are certainly God's Son." Not only did they recognize Jesus as the divine Son of God by the miracle of walking on the water and stopping the storm, but also by stating to His disciples, "I AM." These factors prompted them to respond by immediately worshipping Jesus.

You can imagine the disciples' relief when they realized this was the flesh and blood Jesus in their presence. With that realization, "…they were willing to receive Him into the boat" (vs. 21). At this point, Jesus performed another miracle for His disciples.

The second miracle

The title of this chapter states that miracle #5 is walking on the water. In reality, this miracle is part one of a two-part miracle. The second part is described in the latter half of verse 21 when John includes a unique detail right after Jesus enters the boat, "…immediately the boat was at the land to which they were going." It is unlikely the wind blew them to shore, because Matthew and Mark record that the wind stopped when Jesus entered the boat. Also, at this point in John's narrative, as mentioned above, the disciples were rowing the boat and probably had the sail down. It seems likely that both the wind immediately stopping and the boat immediately arriving at its destination happened simultaneously. We don't know where the boat was located on the sea when Jesus arrived, but John implies that an amazing act took place. This is a miracle because the circumstances would not have allowed for a boat to arrive at its destination without divine intervention immediately. It was more than the providence of God at work. It was beyond physical laws at work. It was a miracle.

Omissions from John's account of this miracle

As mentioned earlier, this account of Jesus walking on the water is described in Matthew, Mark and John. There are two significant details mentioned in Matthew and Mark, but not in John. The first detail was the attempt by Peter to walk on water. This is described in detail by Matthew. The second significant detail was the wind stopping as soon as Jesus entered the boat.

John chose not to include these two elements of the story for a couple reasons. The first reason was because these elements did not add to what John was trying to accomplish. The focus of this miracle was on Jesus in order to further reveal that He is the Christ, the Son of God. This miracle put Jesus's power and authority in a larger context to show His control over basic physical laws by walking on the water. If John had included Peter's failed attempt to walk on water, it would have taken the focus away from Jesus. (Peter's story is an important lesson for each of us to take away. Peter's story showed us what happened when he took his eyes off of Jesus and focused on the storm.) John's narrative was not intended to present a lesson for us to learn. John wanted us to see Jesus, as He is, in a chaotic situation.

The second reason John chose not to include these elements of the story was because they would have been known to most of the readers of his gospel account. Don't forget, Matthew and Mark had already been written several decades before and already had some circulation in the church. You would have thought that including the detail of Jesus stopping the storm would have added to John's goal of showing Jesus as the Son of God. Instead, John considered adding the element of moving the boat immediately to its destination was more significant. It would appear that since stopping the storm was probably well known, John added this component to his story to reinforce the fact that Jesus is sovereign over nature.

John's purpose statement in light of these miracles

Both of these miracles on the stormy sea magnified who Jesus is as the Christ, the Son of God by His control over nature. These miracles show us that His Lordship is beyond healing individual infirmities or feeding huge crowds of people from one small lunch. These miracles are really amazing, but the "stormy sea" miracles show us His Lordship on a grander scale, They show us His control over the whole environment.

These miracles were an opportunity for the disciples and the readers of the book of John to see the ever-expanding reason why we should believe that Jesus is who He says He is. Perhaps trickery could be used by a deceitful person to fake the miracles of Jesus up to this point, but it is not humanly possible to duplicate what Jesus did with these miracles on the Sea of Galilee. Jesus is Lord of all, including the wind and the sea, and He validated that He is indeed the Son of God.

Jesus walking on the water was the first miracle that Jesus had performed that focused on Himself. Jesus did not intend for this focus to be self-serving but to show His authority over the forces of nature. He had already demonstrated this with the previous miracles He had done, but in this case, it was demonstrated dramatically.

With the miracle of the boat immediately reaching its destination, we again see the contrast between human effort and divine power. In the miracle of the feeding of the five thousand, we were able to see the futility of human effort at work to solve the food problem. When proposed human solutions fell short, the problem was solved by divine power. In this miracle we see a more subtle contrast between human effort and divine power. The disciples had spent much of the night rowing and, being curtailed by the storm, were not able to get to their destination. When Jesus arrived on the scene and entered the boat, they immediately arrived at their destination. Who can do these things, except the One who not only claims to be the Son of God, but proves it over and over.

Lessons for us from these miracles

One lesson we learn from these miracles is that Jesus is sovereignly in charge of all things, including the weather. His sovereignty is expressed in the big picture as well as the small details. This tells us that He is in complete control and His concern for us is reflected even in the little things. Jesus demonstrated this with His disciples by showing His sovereign control over the laws of nature and yet, at the same time, showing His concern for them by alleviating their fear. Wouldn't you expect that from an all-powerful, loving God?

A personal example of this was clearly seen by my sister and her husband during Hurricane Ian, when it made landfall on September 28, 2022. They had survived many hurricanes over the years, but they thought this one was going to heavily damage their house. The eye of the storm was just a few miles from their home in Southwest Florida and they watched the water rise higher and higher toward their house from the rain and storm surge. The water level reached the point where it was ready to enter their home and then it stopped rising. The storm had not stopped blowing, but the water level had stopped rising and their home was spared. This was a specific answer to prayer as they saw a loving, sovereign God at work who chose to stop the water from entering their home. This was not a miracle, but God's sovereign hand was at work controlling the storm. Even within the complexity of this Category 4 hurricane, God controlled this small detail of sparing their home from significant damage.

Another lesson from the miracle of walking on the water is found in answering this question: Why were the disciples afraid when they saw Jesus walking on the water? The disciples were surprised to see Jesus walking on the water, which led them to being afraid. He was operating outside of their developing understanding of who they thought Jesus was and what He could do. Don't forget, they still had an incomplete picture of who Jesus was and this miracle fell outside of their perception of Him at this time.

We are no different than the disciples in this respect. We grow in our relationship with others, when we spend time with them and we get to know them. This also applies in our relationship with Christ. Over time, as we get to know Him through the Word of God and walking with Him, we grow in our understanding of who He is. During this process of growth, we should learn to be surprised and not afraid by what Jesus can do in our lives. We should be surprised in the sense that we did not expect or know that He would or could exercise that kind of power and authority in our lives. If we are not surprised by what He is doing in our lives, then perhaps we do not have a complete enough picture of Him to recognize the big things and the little things He is doing.

It is likely we will not have the same experiences the disciples did as they grew in their understanding of Jesus as the Christ, but we will still have experiences that can profoundly affect our relationship with Him.

Chapter 8

MIRACLE #6 IN THE BOOK OF JOHN
HEALING THE MAN, BLIND FROM BIRTH

You have probably heard the saying, "Why do bad things happen to good people?" It is a legitimate question, but not a question we can always answer. Often, the answer is subtle, because the bad thing is causing a transformation in a person's character and relationship with God, which we cannot necessarily see. With the Apostle Paul, he experienced a *thorn in the flesh*, which allowed him to boast about his weaknesses, "…so that the power of Christ may dwell in me" (2 Cor. 12:9). In other words, the *thorn* caused him to be more dependent on Christ.

On other occasions, God causes a person to be afflicted due to their sin. We have already seen that in chapter five, which talks about the healing of the infirmed man who could not walk. In that story, we saw the healing power of Jesus and His authority to forgive sins. On the other side of the coin, God can allow people to be afflicted so that He might show His power and glory in healing that person. This is what we will see with this next miracle of Jesus.

The Gospel of John has over two and a half chapters between miracle #5 and miracle #6. If you have a *red-letter* bible, you will see that Jesus speaks a lot in these chapters. John is showing us what Jesus did and what He taught as He revealed Himself to the people and told them His purpose for being among them. Two significant claims He made about Himself were, "I am the bread of life" (6:35) and "I am the Light of the world" (8:12). We already talked about being the bread of life in chapter 6, but being the light of the world further revealed who He is.

It was during this time, when Jesus was making these hard statements about Himself, that many walked away from His ministry. These people were interested in the benefits of following Jesus, but not willing to commit to what He demanded. A significant statement was made by Peter, when Jesus asked His disciples if they were also going to leave. Peter states, "Lord, to whom shall we go? You have words of eternal life. We have believed and have come to know that You are the Holy One of God" (Jn. 6:68-69). The disciples had developed a solid understanding of who Jesus was and were committing themselves to following Him. As we will see later, their commitment had some cracks in it, but their faith was growing in sharp contrast to those who actively hated and opposed Jesus.

Jesus performed many miracles during His ministry, but John was selective in highlighting only a few of them to demonstrate that Jesus was in fact the Christ (Messiah.) Each miracle showed something about the person of Christ and His authority over all things. The miracles also showed the heart of men and how they responded to the miracles Jesus performed. In John 9, Jesus heals a man who was blind from birth and in this chapter, we will examine the contrasting attitudes and reactions to this miracle.

Setting the scene

We are back in Jerusalem during the Festival of Lights. This is a continuation of John's narrative from chapter eight and it is the last day of the eight-day festival. This festival celebrated the cleansing of the temple and its rededication in 139 B.C., after the Syrian occupiers of Jerusalem had defiled it. According to tradition, a "miracle" occurred, during the time the temple was rededicated, where the lamp in the temple burned for eight days until a new batch of virgin oil could be produced for the lamp. This festival was the context for Jesus talking about being *the Light of the world*. This festival is still celebrated today by the Jews, and it is called Hanukkah, which means "Dedication".

The trigger for this miracle is found in verse two when the disciples and Jesus pass by a man who is blind. Likely the blind man was sitting and begging just outside the temple complex as worshippers were leaving the temple. The disciples ask Jesus a casual question about the man's blindness as they pass by him. Their question reflected a prevailing attitude of that day--he was blind due to his sin or the sins of the parents. This was the same attitude Job's friends had towards Job when he experienced all of his misfortune. They assumed that Job had sinned and God was judging him for the sin. We know this was not true in Job's case and Jesus also made it clear it was not true with the blind man. In both cases, the misfortune was allowed to happen so God could receive the glory. The Godhead sovereignly planned this divine appointment with the blind man. From eternity past, it was determined that this man would be born blind, and he would be at the right place at the right time to have an encounter with Jesus. We don't learn anything more about the disciples' attitude after the miracle occurs, but no doubt they learned a lot as they saw the events unfold from their one casual question.

This miracle was unusual because the person was not healed immediately. He had to obey Jesus in order to see his sight gained. Jesus applied mud to the blind man's eyes and then told him to go to the Pool of Siloam[1] and wash the mud off his eyes. It was at this point, when he washed the mud off his eyes, that his sight was gained. The mud was not intended to have some medicinal affect, but to test the man's commitment to have his sight gained. The man could have created all kinds of excuses for not washing the mud off his eyes, but he stepped out in faith, trusting the words of Jesus.

The question arises how the blind man found his way to the Pool of Siloam since he had been blind since birth. The pool was about seven-hundred yards from the south gate of the temple mount and archeologists have found broad steps at the Pool of Siloam, which they call ascent stairs or the Pilgrimage Road which leads directly to the temple complex. The blind man could have negotiated the ascent stairs by himself or perhaps he had the help of a companion. However he got to the pool, he acted in obedience and faith.

Jesus had spoken of being the Light of the world in verse five and now He illustrated it with this miracle. Here is a man who was physically in darkness all of his life and when his eyes were opened, he experienced the light. The wonderful part of this story, as we will discuss later, is that this same man was also in spiritual darkness and then he experienced the Light of the world and believed.

The religious response

The first response we see on full display is the religious response of the Pharisees. It is so ugly to see their reaction to this miracle and the utter contempt they had towards the healed man and his parents. They are so intimidating and condescending towards them. Verse 35 best shows their attitude, "They [Pharisees] answered him [the healed man], "You were born entirely in sins, and are you teaching us?" So, "they put him out." We could say this attitude was born out of Jesus healing on the Sabbath (again), but this miracle showed the continual hardening of their hearts. Jesus had made mud for the blind man's eyes and the Pharisees considered this labor. Jesus had broken their definition of keeping the Sabbath and they could not see before them, the One who had given the Law to the children of Abraham. This completely clouded their thinking about how a man who was blind from birth could gain his sight, even when he is standing before them. Their man-made religion kept them from seeing Jesus.

The social pressure response

The second response we see in this chapter is the social pressure response. This is expressed by the healed man's parents in verses 18-22. You would expect the parents to be excited over the healing of their son, but they were "…afraid of the Jews…" (vs. 22). In other words, their standing in the community was more important than their son's eyesight. They did not want to get kicked out of the synagogue, which was more than a religious meeting place. It also had the function of a community center. They did not want to be ostracized by this social group. You can see in their discussion with the Jews they were trying to deflect any attention away from themselves to avoid anything from happening to them. In the modern vernacular, they "threw their son under the bus." Their faith revolved around the religious and social constructs of the culture and not in the Messiah, who had healed their son.

The seeker's response

The last response, and I saved the best for last, was the seeker's response as seen with the healed man. His faith and testimony was so simple, it confounded the religious leaders. All he could do was testify to what had happened to him. The problem the Pharisees had with this man is that they could not refute what happened to him. He was clearly blind from birth and now he can see. When the healed man saw Jesus again (vss. 35-38), his faith was made complete when he found out that Jesus is the Son of Man. I love the healed man's response in verse 38, "And he said, "Lord, I believe." And he worshiped Him." The healed man immediately recognized Jesus as the Messiah and Lord and his first act of faith was worshipping his Savior.

If you remember from chapter two of this book, I commented on the phrase, *believe in,* as an indication of a person's total commitment, "…to the person of Christ as Messiah and Lord…" This phrase was used by the healed man when he asked Jesus the question, "Who is He, Lord, that I may *believe in* Him?" (vs. 36). The man was ready to be all in for Christ. He just needed to know who Christ was. As we have seen above, when he found out that Jesus was the Christ, He demonstrated his total commitment.

We are able to see, as this story developed, how the blind man, who was healed, grew in his understanding of Jesus. His understanding culminated in believing and worshipping Him.

John's purpose statement in light of this miracle

What is to be learned from this miracle, particularly when we see the different responses to it? In John 20, John's purpose statement states, "…that they might believe."

John is using a Greek mood here, called the subjunctive, to indicate an element of doubt. In other words, a person exposed to the claims and miracles of Christ *may or may not* believe. This miracle shows the subjunctive played out. For the healed man, his faith came out of being healed and recognizing the Messiah as the one who healed him. For the healed man's parents and the Pharisees, they were driven by their desires and reputations. Because they were concerned about themselves, this undisputed miracle could not draw them to their Messiah. As we reflect upon our own lives, it has to be God drawing us for us to see who He is.

This miracle reinforces Jesus's teaching that He is the Light of the world. By giving sight to this man, Jesus showed that he had been physically blind all of his life and then saw light for the first time. This is in contrast to those who had physical sight for their whole lives yet were spiritually blind. By healing the blind man, Jesus shows He is capable of bringing spiritual and physical light to people. This is exactly what the blind man experienced.

Lessons for us from this miracle

In the story of the miracle with the royal official's son, we got to see the official's spiritual journey culminate in genuine faith in Christ. In the story of the blind man, we go on the same spiritual journey. One big difference between the two stories is the starting point of the blind man's journey. The royal official actively pursued Jesus, hoping that Jesus could heal his son. The blind man had probably heard some things about Jesus from overhearing the conversations of people passing by him, but having an encounter with Jesus likely never entered his mind. John included a lot of details around this miracle so that we might see the steps this blind man took to come to faith in Christ.

The first step in the blind man's faith journey was simple obedience. It must have been amazing to the blind man that Jesus had singled him out, particularly as he heard the conversation between Jesus and His disciples. Jesus commanded him to wash the mud off his eyes, which were strange and challenging commands, but the blind man obeyed without asking any questions. It seems likely that the man's obedience was sparked by Jesus saying, "It was neither that this man sinned, nor his parents; but it was so that the works of God might be displayed in him" (vs. 3). After being bombarded all of his life with the common notion that his state of blindness was due to sin, Jesus's statement must have planted a seed of hope in him.

The next step we see in the blind man's faith journey is allowing the facts of his testimony guide him. He first demonstrated this when his neighbors and others who saw him were confused because they knew him as being blind, and now, he can see. His testimony was very simple, and he only communicated what he knew. His testimony was 1) identifying the author of the miracle, 2) explaining the process for the miracle to occur and 3) the result of the miracle. This simple testimony was then challenged during his first encounter with the Pharisees. Their focus was not on the miracle of gaining sight, but on the credibility of the one who healed him. During this encounter we could see the healed man's faith take a step forward when the Pharisees asked, "What do you say, about Him, since he opened your eyes?" (vs. 17). He recognized that the one who healed him was no ordinary person; therefore, he considered Him a prophet. At this point in his journey, this was the conclusion he had drawn.

The third step in his faith journey was when he had his second meeting with the Pharisees. During this encounter the healed man applied theological logic based upon what he knew about God. Don't forget, this man was talking with religious experts, but their problem was they were spiritually blind religious experts. With the healed man's undeniable testimony of sight as his basis, he explained to them that only someone from God could give sight to the blind, because, "we know that God does not hear sinners…" (vs. 31). As he is thinking through what has happened to him and how it could happen, he is drawing correct conclusions.

The Pharisees did not have a response for the healed man because he was theologically correct. As so often happens, when an opponent has no rebuttal to an argument they will resort to *ad hominem* attacks. The Pharisees were no different as they tried to assert their intellectual superiority by saying, "You were born entirely in sin and are you teaching us?" (vs. 34). The healed man was not trying to teach the Pharisees, but was growing in his understanding of who it was who healed him.

The final step of the healed man's faith journey was believing in Jesus as the Christ, the Son of God. This occurred when Jesus found the man and asked him, "Do you believe in the Son of Man?" (vs. 35). At this point, when Jesus identified Himself as the Son of Man, all the pieces of the puzzle came together for the healed man and he believed. He was totally committed and he demonstrated the genuineness of his faith through worshipping Jesus.

For those of you who are followers of Christ, each of you have had a faith journey, just like the healed man, that led you to Jesus. I can guarantee you that none of your faith journeys were like his or like each other's. Our faith journey is unique, but there are at least three elements we have in common with the healed man in our journey.

1) Jesus meets us where we are. This was clearly seen with the blind man. This man did not have a clear understanding of who Jesus was and he certainly was not seeking Him. Jesus sought him out, when He orchestrated the man's healing. He sought him out again after he had gained his sight which led him to believing in Jesus. Clearly, Jesus did not impose any preconditions upon the man, but accepted him as he was. As followers of Christ, He accepted us where we were at spiritually as we began our spiritual journey. Some of you already had a sense of who Jesus was and others of you had no exposure to Him or even utterly rejected Jesus. Fortunately, Jesus did not expect us to clean up our lives first before He met us. Instead, He met us as sinners and guided us to salvation in Him.

2) God orchestrates the events to draw us to Himself. John recorded how the blind man moved from spiritual blindness to spiritual sight through the events in his life, which were outlined above. Some of us may have had many events for years that brought us to Christ, and for others, it may have happened very quickly. Again, God is at work in our lives as individuals, not with a "cookie-cutter" approach. Fortunately, God has given us "20/20 hindsight" to see those events that led us to Christ.

3) We must believe in Jesus. The two common elements described above culminated in the healed man believing in Jesus. In the same way, God was at work in our lives, leading us to a saving knowledge of Jesus. Paul describes this process of being saved in Titus 3:5-6, "He saved us, not based on deeds which we have done in righteousness, but according to His mercy, by the washing of regeneration and renewing by the Holy Spirit, whom He poured out upon us richly through Jesus Christ our Savior." Whereas believing in Jesus entails a total commitment on our part, this passage shows the work of the Triune Godhead in bringing us to that total commitment. It is easy to see why the healed man worshipped Jesus as his first act of commitment.

There are two other lessons we can derive from this story, which are practical for each follower of Christ. The first lesson is to recognize that each of us has a testimony. The healed man's testimony was simple, and he used it effectively. Our testimony can be simple and effective, also. Our testimony is in three parts, 1) my life before Christ, 2) how I accepted Christ as my Savior, and 3) my life after Christ. That was, in essence, the testimony of the healed man before the Pharisees. What we saw through this story was the healed man's testimony become more developed, particularly when he believed in Jesus. Here is a challenge for each reader of this section: put together your testimony, covering the three sections outlined above, and confine the content so you can present it in 1-2 minutes. We can always expand our testimony, but a 1–2-minute testimony will ensure you have the essential elements covered.

The last lesson to be learned from this miracle is from the response of the parents. As discussed above, their response to the Pharisees was dictated by social pressure rather than the truth. In other words, their priorities were on display. Their number one priority was their standing in the community and their son was somewhere down the list. We may find ourselves in situations where our faith in Christ is highlighted by others. The question is how do we respond in those situations? These situations always show us and others the priority Christ has in our lives. This is often a good time to share our testimony which we have already prepared from the previous lesson.

This story of the blind man gaining his sight shows how divisive Jesus was when He was on the earth. The story is no different today. Jesus is divisive in our world, even though He came to be the Savior of the world.

The spiritual lesson from this miracle

The theme of blindness and sight in this story goes beyond physical blindness and sight. We have seen how the blind man gained both physical and spiritual sight from Jesus and now Jesus is making a more significant point in verses 39-41. John is not simply recounting events, but is making a point through this story. In this case, Jesus is pointing out that He did not come into the world to judge it, but to show man their sin.

John concludes this story with Jesus commenting about spiritual sight and blindness with the Pharisees. Again, they do not understand what He is saying and they ask Him if He thinks they are blind. The point Jesus makes in verse 41 is that if we are completely blind spiritually, then we would have no sense of sin. This is not the reality with humans. We have some sense of sight through our conscience, or self-made law we have created, or God's Law. He is telling the Pharisees that since you claim to have sight you still have sin. In other words, you have the Messiah, the Son of God before you and yet you are in sin, because you are rejecting Him.

I think you can imagine how the Pharisees reacted internally and perhaps externally, when Jesus made this statement. Being self-deceived by their religion and thinking they are religious, they believe they have spiritual sight, but in reality, they are spiritually blind. They cannot see their true spiritual condition, and when, "the Way, the Truth and the Life" (Jn. 14:6) is before them, they see Him as the enemy.

Perhaps some of you reading this are in the same situation as the Pharisees. You think you have spiritual sight because you are religious or you are a good person, but like the Pharisees, you are spiritually blind. I trust, as you continue reading about the miracles Jesus performed, you will see Jesus as He really is, the Christ, the Son of God and you may believe in His name.

---

[1] The Pool of Siloam was located south of the temple complex in a section of Jerusalem called the City of David. Like the Pool of Bethesda, the Pool of Siloam was originally a water reservoir, which later became a *mikveh,* a place for ceremonial cleansing. This makes sense why the Pilgrimage Road, mentioned in the chapter, was built. This allowed for the "clean" Jewish pilgrims to ascend to the temple mount without accidentally becoming unclean. Ironically, the word Siloam is from a Hebrew word for *sent*, which is exactly what Jesus did with the blind man to get the mud washed off his eyes. For more information on the Pool of Siloam, I would recommend the article by Bryant G. Wood, titled, *Extraordinary Excavations: The Pilgrimage Road and the Pool of Siloam* found in biblearchaeology.com.

Chapter 9

Miracle #7 in the Book of John
Raising Lazarus from the Dead

One of the most difficult things we will experience in life is the death of a loved one. Death is inevitable for us as humans, therefore, each of us will likely go through the mourning process for someone who was close to us. Followers of Christ will mourn also, even though we know that our loved ones who followed Christ are in the presence of the Lord. One reason death is so difficult to deal with is because it was not a part of what God intended when He created the heavens and the earth. When Adam and Eve rebelled against God in the garden, death was introduced into the world and it has been a part of life ever since. In other words, death is an unnatural abnormality that was introduced into the world by sin and now it seems normal. We will observe with the miracle, concerning Lazarus, how the pain and emotion of death even affects Jesus, the Creator of the world (see John 1:3).

As we see John present the miracles of Jesus, there is a sense that the significance of each miracle is building. It feels like we are coming to a climax with the miracles, which is the case, because we are on the verge of seeing the most significant miracle in the Gospel of John--the resurrection of Jesus from the dead. The miracle that prepares us for the resurrection of Jesus is the resuscitation of Lazarus from the dead. The word, resuscitation is deliberately used because Lazarus will have to face death again after Jesus calls him out of the tomb. From here on out, I will use the term, raised, instead of resuscitation, but you will know what I mean when I speak of Lazarus rising from the dead. My finite imagination wonders what Lazarus experienced those four days when he was dead. I wonder if he was disappointed to be brought back to this earth when Jesus called him out of the tomb? These are questions we will have answered when we see Lazarus in heaven.

The raising of Lazarus is the third time that Jesus raised someone from the dead. The other two events were the raising of the widow's son in the city of Nain, found in Luke 7:11-19 and the raising of Jairus' daughter in Capernaum, found in Luke 8:40-42; 49-56. What makes the raising of Lazarus different from these accounts is:

- The amount of space given by John to record the event. Even though verse divisions came much later in the transmission of the Bible, it is helpful here to see that John devoted forty-four verses to this miracle.

- Jesus had a personal relationship with the key figures in this miracle. In contrast, Jesus only met the widow in passing as He was entering Nain and Jesus met Jairus only because Jairus came to Him concerning his daughter.

- We get to see the humanity of Jesus in a very personal way. The focus of this story was not on the miracle of raising Lazarus alone, but also on Jesus's human interactions with Lazarus's sisters.

- We also see the deep emotions which Jesus expressed. Most young bible students are familiar with the shortest verse in the English Bible, "Jesus wept" (Jn. 11:35). This is an example of the emotion Jesus felt over the death of his close friend.

- This story is developed over several days because there is more involved with the narrative than just the miracle alone. The encounter with the widow occurred in the moment, and the raising of Jairus' daughter happened over a few hours.

- Finally, Jesus clearly states the purposes of this miracle to His disciples prior to its happening. This miracle is "…for the glory of God…" (Jn. 11:4) and "…so that you may believe…" (vs. 15).

Setting the scene

The story of Lazarus raised from the dead is only recorded in the Gospel of John and is found in John 11:1-44. Many of the other miracles involved individuals whom Jesus had come upon or who were brought to him. Lazarus, on the other hand, was a personal friend. Jesus closely connected with Lazarus and his sisters, Mary and Martha. This is evident by the number of times it says in the text that He loved them as close friends (see vs. 5 as an example)[1]. John also clarifies for his readers who Mary was in verse two, with a parenthetical statement about her anointing Jesus with ointment. The question arises as to whether John is talking about the person mentioned in Luke 7:38 or Mary, clearly identified in John 12:3. It seems likely John is referring to the anointing by Mary in John twelve. Even though this took place after Lazarus was raised from the dead, Mary's anointing of Jesus was also recorded by Matthew (Mt. 26:6-13) and Mark (Mk. 14:3-9), though she was not named in those accounts. Most of the readers of John's account would have already been familiar with the story from the other gospel accounts[2].

The story of this miracle begins with Jesus and His disciples located beyond the Jordan River. They were at Bethany (see Jn. 1:28), where John the Baptist baptized people. Ironically, Lazarus also lived in Bethany, but his village was less than two miles from Jerusalem. The Bethany where Jesus was at was around eighty miles away from Jerusalem. The reason Jesus was staying in Bethany was to get away from the Jews who were trying to kill him. Jesus was not being secretive about staying at Bethany because many people were coming to see Him and "Many believed in Him there" (Jn. 10:42). Understanding where Jesus was located helps us to gain insights into the story around the miracle.

We immediately find out that Lazarus is sick in verse one and it appears to be very serious because someone is sent to Jesus to report about Lazarus's condition. The seriousness of his sickness is amplified by the fact that the messenger traveled about eighty miles to deliver the message. Though it is not stated, it is implied that the sisters were hoping that Jesus would heal their brother, either remotely, like with the royal official's son, or would come quickly to heal him in person.

Jesus's response to the news

Upon hearing the news of His friend's illness, we would have expected Jesus to act quickly and take the necessary steps to heal his friend. Instead, He "...stayed two days *longer* in the place where He was" (vs. 6). Clearly, Jesus was not caught off guard by the news, because His plans were greater than Lazarus's current need. He saw it as an opportunity, "...for the glory of God, so that the Son of God may be glorified by it" (vs. 4). Jesus was wanting God's will, not their will, to be done.

As Jesus responded to the news, the disciples clearly did not understand what was going on. During the two days Jesus waited before heading out to Bethany, the disciples were likely confident that Jesus was going to take care of things with Lazarus. When Jesus was ready to go see His friend, the response of the disciples focused on safety, not Lazarus. Their response to His plan is understood because this was the reason they were staying beyond the Jordan and now He wants to head back into imminent danger. Jesus responded to their concern, in verses 9-10, with a cryptic answer that had a physical and spiritual aspect to it. The light of day He is describing has the sense of, "During my limited twelve hours of 'daytime' labor, I am focused on doing my Father's will and so I will never lack his protection (to stumble)"[3]. In other words, Jesus was not concerned with the danger, because He knew God's hand of protection was upon Him to complete God's will while it is still day.

The disciples were further confused when Jesus tells them that Lazarus is asleep. They interpret this to mean that Lazarus is recovering from his illness. This further amplified their confusion as to why they needed to travel back to see him. They are likely thinking that the health crisis has passed and whether they still want to head back into a potentially dangerous situation? Jesus then clarified Lazarus's situation by clearly telling the disciples that he is dead. He also implicitly explains why He delayed their departure and allowed Lazarus to die; "…that you may believe…" (vs. 15).

Thomas provides a pessimistic response to Jesus's travel plans. His focus and likely the focus of many of the other disciples, was on what they may face when they return. Their faith in Jesus has grown during their time with Him, but there is still a practical element in their thinking that overrides the fact that they are with the Son of God and He is in control of the situation.

In spite of their less than enthusiastic response towards travelling back to Judea, the disciples did accompany Jesus on this trip. As noted earlier, Jesus and the disciples were located about eighty miles from the home of Lazarus and his sisters in Bethany. This meant that it was about a four-day trip to get to Bethany. They left when Jesus revealed to His disciples that Lazarus was dead, which means Lazarus had been dead for four days when they arrived on the scene.

Jesus' response to the sisters

When Jesus and the disciples arrived, Lazarus had already been placed in the tomb. Because the climate was warmer in this region, deceased individuals were quickly prepared for burial and were either buried in the ground or placed in a tomb. They did not embalm the body, but wrapped it in strips of cloth and placed spices between the layers of fabric. Lazarus' sisters were mourning for their brother, and the mourners included "…many of the Jews…" (vs. 19) who had come from Jerusalem. This tells us about the respect and regard this family had in the Jewish community.

It should be noted that Lazarus and his sisters were not just friends of Jesus, but also followers of Jesus. This is clearly stated in verse 27, when Martha says to Jesus, "…I have believed that You are the Christ, the Son of God…" Martha stated that she believed in Him and currently believes in Him. This is important as we see how the sisters interact with Jesus.

Martha was the first to interact with Jesus upon His arrival. She went out to meet Him as He was coming to Bethany. Martha showed her faith in Jesus by responding to Him with confidence. She believed Jesus could do whatever He wished. She wished He could have been there before her brother died, but is not disappointed by His late arrival. We see her faith in Jesus is still limited, because when Jesus said to her, "Your brother will rise again" (vs. 23), she was only thinking of a future resurrection, not the possibility of seeing him rise this day. As Jesus makes another "I am" statement to Martha in verses 25-26, her thoughts are still towards a future resurrection of her brother.

At this point, Martha calls for her sister, Mary, to come and see Jesus. When Mary sees Jesus, she reveres Him by falling at His feet. By her veneration towards Jesus, she recognized Him, as Martha did, as the Christ, the Son of God. Then Mary conveys the same message as Martha, wishing He had arrived on time. Seeing Mary and the Jews with her weeping caused a deep stirring of emotion within Jesus. One of the emotions Jesus expressed was sorrow over the death of a good friend. This sorrow would include the heartache Mary and Martha are experiencing. The Jews on the scene also noticed Jesus's emotional response and noted, "See how He loved him!" (vs. 36). This was not the only reason Jesus had a deep, emotional response to this tragedy.

Jesus's response to death

This is such an amazing story, as we witness the deep emotion expressed by Jesus. In other stories, we see it stated that Jesus "...felt compassion..." (see Mt. 14:14, for example), but in this account, we see the physical expression of His emotion. We are familiar with the shortest verse in the Bible, "Jesus wept" (vs. 25), but another emotion Jesus expresses during this story is not as easily seen in most English translations of the Bible. In verses 33 and 38 it says that Jesus was "...deeply moved..." within. In the context of the passage, we would assume that Jesus was experiencing deep grief over the loss of His friend, but the emotion that Jesus was actually feeling was anger/displeasure/indignation. This emotion is further amplified in verse 33, "He [Jesus] was deeply moved in spirit and was troubled." This emotion was deeply internalized and not the type of emotion you would expect from someone who has lost his friend. It does beg the question: What made Jesus so angry?

The text does not explicitly say, but the context gives us some strong hints. His anger was much larger than the death of his friend. What triggered His anger in verse 33 was seeing Mary, and the Jews with her, weeping. In verse 38, His anger was triggered again as they approached the tomb where his deceased friend was laid. It appears His anger was over death itself and seeing the consequences of death with His dear friend. Death was never God's plan but was introduced into His creation with the sin of Adam and Eve. Jesus, the creator of the world (John 1:3), was personally seeing the devastating effect of sin and death upon the world. We certainly understand this response in our own lives. When we hear about the death of hundreds of people in another part of the world, due to a natural disaster, it impacts us, but usually in a superficial way. When we hear of the death of a close friend or loved one, it pierces deep within us. Jesus's response is reflective of His humanity as the God/man.

Jesus's response to Lazarus

The story does not end here. In fact, we get the sense that the story is coming to a dramatic climax as Jesus responds to the impact that death has had, not only on Mary and Martha, but the whole world. Lazarus had been dead for four days and in the minds of the Jews he was really dead. We associate permanence with physical death because people do not become alive again after they are dead. On the other hand, Jesus saw Lazarus as asleep and His plan, from the beginning of this story, was to awaken him out of his sleep (see verse 11). This understanding of Jesus's plan to "awaken" Lazarus does not undermine the emotion Jesus was feeling, as described above.

A crowd was present at the tomb when Jesus prepared to raise Lazarus. No one knew what was going to happen next. They assumed that Jesus was simply there to continue mourning for His friend. Imagine the surprise, when Jesus said, "Remove the stone" (vs. 39). It must have been disconcerting to the crowd to hear this because Lazarus was dead. Martha pointed out the obvious, "…there will be a stench…" (vs. 39). Jesus assures them that they will see the glory of God, if they believe (vs. 40). The next step was significant. They removed the stone.

Jesus could have easily spectacularly removed the stone Himself, but he wanted it removed by some of the men present. Everyone could have dismissed this command as foolish and then ridiculed Jesus for making such a request, but instead, they complied. This act on their part was a way for them to show, outwardly, that they believed they would see the glory of God at work.

Jesus wanted to make sure the crowd knew the source of this miracle. He does this by calling out to God the Father. Jesus ensured the crowd saw the connection between Himself and His Father. Then Jesus demonstrated His authority over death by crying loudly, "Lazarus, come forth" (vs. 43). Lazarus came out of that tomb, raised from the dead. Lazarus had the same body that went into that tomb four days ago and was still wrapped up. I imagine it was difficult for him to shuffle out of the tomb. Again, Jesus could have had him come out with the wrappings already off of him, but this created a clear picture that he was dead and is now alive.

This miracle was so mighty that "many of the Jews who came to Mary, and saw what He had done, believed in Him" (vs. 45). This miracle also had a negative impact. The religious leaders, continuing to see the threat Jesus posed because more and more people believed in Him, decided to expand the scope of their plot. They determined to not only kill Jesus, but also kill Lazarus "…because on account of him many of the Jews were going away and were believing in Jesus" (Jn. 12:10-11).

John's purpose statement in light of this miracle

As mentioned at the beginning of this chapter, this miracle was the perfect prelude to Jesus rising from the dead. Lazarus arose only to face death again someday. Jesus would occur, having destroyed sin and death on the cross three days before. The miracle of Lazarus provided a compelling reason to believe that, "…Jesus is the Christ, the Son of God." If Jesus can and did conquer the final enemy, death, then, by, "…believing you may have life in His name."

By now, you have probably noticed that Jesus uses the phrase "believe in" three times in this story, in verses 25, 26, and 45. If we are going to experience life, even if we die, then it requires a total commitment to Him. The word "believe" is also mentioned three times in this account, in verses 15, 27, and 40.

The focus of this miracle is best described by Jesus's statement to Martha, "I am the resurrection and the life; he who believes in Me will live even if he dies…" (vs. 25). It is easy to make claims about yourself without backing it up, but Jesus's claim about His authority over life and death was demonstrated with the rising of Lazarus. Jesus clearly showed He was from God and was the Son of God. It makes sense, then, why John included this miracle in the Gospel of John.

A lesson for us from this miracle

How many times have you heard it stated at a funeral that this is a "celebration of life"? There is truth to this statement, if the one being remembered was a follower of Christ and is now in the presence of the Lord. At the same time, there is still an underlying feeling of grief and loss because the loved one is not physically with us. After my first wife died of cancer in her mid-20s, I remember my grandma saying to me, "Isn't it better she is in heaven? You wouldn't want her back to continue suffering." I agreed with her, but...I still missed her presence in my life. This pain we experience with the loss of a loved one is all part of the human experience, because God created us to be relational.

I mention this because it is okay to mourn and cry over the death of our loved ones, even the ones who are with the Lord in heaven. Jesus mourned over the death of Lazarus, not only because he was a close friend, but also because He felt the tragedy and the destruction that sin and death had brought to the world. This was particularly intense for Jesus because He knew what the creation was like before sin entered the world and now, He is personally experiencing its destructive nature. Even though Jesus knew that He was going to reconcile the world in a short time with His death, burial and resurrection from the dead, the current situation was still a wrenching experience for Him.

As we go through the mourning process for a loved one, we know Jesus is there to comfort us because He knows what mourning for a loved one feels like. In Hebrews 4:15-16, it states, "For we do not have a high priest who cannot sympathize with our weaknesses, but One who has been tempted in all things as *we are, yet* without sin. Therefore, let us draw near with confidence to the throne of grace, so that we may receive mercy and find grace to help in time of need." This verse describes Jesus, being fully human, was able to experience the same life experiences that every human goes through, including temptations. He personally understands us. That is why we can find "…grace and mercy…" from Him in our time of need. That time of need includes mourning the loss of a loved one.

This is the last of the seven miracles which John chose to highlight in the Gospel of John. These seven miracles performed by Jesus were to show the Jews who He was and the authority He had over the physical universe. We will do a wrap up of these miracles and their significance in chapter eleven, but there is one more miracle to be covered which was the most significant sign of them all; the resurrection of Jesus from the dead. The seven miracles we have covered were designed to point the audience to Him as the Christ, the Son of God, but this last miracle was done to open the way to eternal life through Him.

ADDENDUM

At the beginning of the chapter, it was mentioned that this miracle was like a climax, preparing us for Jesus' resurrection from the dead. Not only does the story itself lead us to that conclusion, but there are many parallels between the raising of Lazarus and the resurrection of Jesus. They are parallels in the sense that Lazarus' rising from the dead points us to something so much greater in Jesus's resurrection. The following is a table outlining those parallels.

The raising of Lazarus	The resurrection of Jesus Christ
He arose from the dead, BUT had to die again	He arose from the dead, never to die again
He kept his corruptible body, subject to mortality	He received an incorruptible body, glorified, perfect and immortal
He was buried in a cave with a stone rolled over the entrance	He was buried in a cave with a stone rolled over the entrance
The stone was taken away by a group of men	The stone was taken away by divine power
Jesus called out to Lazarus to come forth from the tomb	Jesus came out of the tomb by His own power and authority

Lazarus was placed in the grave bound from head to foot with grave wrappings	Jesus was placed in the grave bound from head to foot with grave wrappings
Lazarus left the tomb under his own power, though with a shuffle.	Jesus left the tomb in a glorious way, leaving those guarding the tomb stunned.
Lazarus needed to have his grave wrappings removed by others	Jesus's grave wrappings were left in the tomb, in the place where His body laid.
Many believed that Jesus is the Messiah, the Son of God	Many are believing, to this day, that Jesus is the Christ, the Son of God.

---

[1] I want to clarify any confusion I might have caused by saying that Jesus loved them as close friends. When you read your English translation or the Greek text, it does not say that. This idea of love as friends is implied by the words John uses to describe Jesus's love for these siblings. John uses the verb form of the words *phileō* (vs. 3, 36) and *agapē* (vs. 5), to describe the love Jesus had for Lazarus. John had the habit, in his gospel account, to use similar words interchangeably, as part of his writing style, to provide variety in the text. This is what John was doing here with the two words for love. If we combine the ideas of love as a commitment (*agapē*) and love that reciprocates *(phileō)*, you get the sense of the type of love Jesus had for these siblings. Finally, it should be noted that John used the noun form, *philos*, in verse 11 when Jesus stated, "Our friend [philos] Lazarus has fallen asleep…" This reinforces their relationship as friends.

[2] It should also be noted that another anointing, recorded in Luke seven, occurred in Galilee. It seems unlikely that Mary, the sister of Lazarus, would have been in Galilee, let alone have an expensive box of perfume available to anoint Jesus at that time. Though the anointings are very similar, the person in the Luke account is not named and is unknown to us, though you are guaranteed to hear speculations around her identity.

[3] Murray Harris, John in *Exegetical Guide to the Greek New Testament* (Nashville: B&H Publishing, 2015), p. 209.

Chapter 10

THE ULTIMATE MIRACLE IN THE BOOK OF JOHN THE RESURRECTION OF JESUS FROM THE DEAD

The most destructive war in mankind's history was World War II. Even though it lasted six years, it is estimated that fifteen million military personnel and thirty-eight million civilians died in the war[1]. My math comes up with fifty-three million human beings, from over thirty countries, perished in this war. One technology that was used extensively during the war was the airplane. The bomber had a massive impact in destroying the enemy's military, industrial, and logistical infrastructures. It was from these bombing runs that millions of civilians were also killed.

Even though thousands upon thousands of bombs were dropped during World War II, there was a game-changer that occurred on August 6, 1945. A bomb named Little Boy was dropped upon Hiroshima, Japan and the world was forever changed. Of course, Little Boy was the first atomic bomb dropped upon a population. The casualties were estimated to be between 90,000 and 160,000 people, from the initial blast and the later effects of radiation poisoning.[2] The destructive force of Little Boy was equivalent to fifteen kilotons of TNT. Another atomic bomb was dropped on Nagasaki three days later, and Japan surrendered on August 16. Fortunately, there has not been another nuclear bomb dropped upon a population since then.

This introduction is a bit gruesome, but it illustrates how significant an event can be when there have been hundreds and thousands of similar events before this single event. Even today, armies are still bombing other armies using airplanes, rockets and missiles, but there have still been only these two atomic bombs dropped.

When we consider the miracles that Jesus performed during His earthly ministry, they certainly impacted individuals and groups of people. One miracle was far and away more significant than any other miracle that Jesus performed. This was His resurrection from the dead. The miracles Jesus performed and the other miracles found in the Bible are equivalent to a conventional bomb. His resurrection from the dead is like a hydrogen bomb in comparison. The two significant differences in this comparison are 1) His miracles were not destructive, and 2) His resurrection had an eternal impact which affected the whole world, positively, even to this day.

Setting the scene

We now come to the most critical miracle performed by Jesus. As you would easily guess, the crucifixion, burial and resurrection of Jesus are recorded in all four gospel accounts. After all, this was the primary purpose for Jesus coming to this earth--to be crucified as a substitutionary death for the sins of the whole world. Jesus made it very clear this was His purpose when He stated to His disciples, in the midst of His public ministry that, "From that time Jesus began to show His disciples that he must go to Jerusalem, and suffer many things from the elders and chief priests and scribes, and be killed, and be raised up on the third day" (Mt. 16:21). Even though He stated this many times, the disciples were still not ready for this to take place. In fact, John was the only disciple who personally witnessed the crucifixion of Jesus. The others were likely in hiding for fear of the Jews (see Jn. 20:19).

As mentioned before, all four gospel accounts tell the story of the resurrection and post-resurrection events of Jesus. We will only focus on the details that John recorded in Jn. 20:1-29. Some of the story overlaps with the other gospel accounts, but there are many details unique to John. We will examine how different individuals and one group of people responded to the news of His resurrection.

Mary Magdalene's response to the resurrection

The first person mentioned by John, who arrived at the empty tomb, was Mary Magdalene. She was there on the first day of the week and got there before the sun had risen. Even though it was still dark, she knew where to go because she had observed where the burial party had laid the body of Jesus on Friday (see Mk. 15:47) after He was crucified. The tomb was located in a garden and not a cemetery; therefore, she would not have gotten mixed up and gone to the wrong tomb. Other gospel accounts also mention that Mary was not alone. There were other women that went with Mary Magdalene to the tomb with spices for the body of Jesus. John decides to only highlight Mary Magdalene because she becomes a part of his story of highlighting the post-resurrection appearances of Jesus.

There are three important facts to point out about Mary Magdalene's relationship with Jesus. The first and most important fact is that she was delivered from seven demons (Lk. 8:2). There is not a description of the actual event in the gospel accounts, but there are stories of others who were delivered from demons. These stories can give us a sense of what Mary might have been going through before she was delivered. She became a fully committed follower of Jesus and she was one of many who followed Him in His ministry. She was able to follow Jesus from town to town because she was a person of some means and was able to finance her travels. The second important fact is that Mary had enough money to also help in the support of Jesus's ministry. Mary

Magdalene was one of "...many others who were contributing to their [Jesus and the disciples] support out of their private means" (Lk. 8:3). The third important fact is that Mary Magdalene was present at the crucifixion of Jesus. She was not alone at the crucifixion, but was with other women, including the mother of Jesus (Jn. 19:25-26).

This was who Mary Magdalene was, and it makes sense that she would be at the empty tomb of Jesus on that Easter morning. Before we look at her encounter with Jesus, let me state that she was called Mary Magdalene because she was from the town of Magdala, which was located on the western shore of the Sea of Galilee. She was likely called Mary Magdalene to help distinguish her from the other women, called Mary, that are mentioned in the gospel accounts.

We already noted that Mary Magdalene and other women were the first ones at the empty tomb of Jesus. From the synoptic gospels, we learn that two angels were present to tell the women that Jesus had risen and to go tell the disciples to meet Him in Galilee. Upon hearing this, all the women ran back to tell the disciples. From John's account, it appears that Mary was not convinced that Jesus was risen. Based upon the physical evidence which Mary observed, His body was taken and this is what she communicated to the disciples (Jn. 20:2).

In verse 18 of John's account, we find Mary back at the tomb of Jesus after Peter and John had already come to the tomb and left. We don't know if she went with Peter and John when they ran to the tomb or if she travelled alone, but she was now there alone. We learn a lot about Mary Magdalene from her unexpected encounter with Jesus in John 20:11-18.

First, we see that Mary was focused. Her focus was on the finding the body of Jesus and properly preparing the body. We clearly see this by her outpouring of emotion and her response to the angels and the "gardener" when they ask her why is she weeping (vs. 13-15). It does not appear that Mary is taken aback by talking to angels because she had already encountered them earlier, when she was at the tomb the first time. Her focus was on finding the body of Jesus.

Second, we see Mary's focus expressed by her persistence and boldness. Her persistence is seen by coming back to the tomb a second time. She was determined to find the body of Jesus. Her boldness was expressed by being at the tomb by herself. She did not show fear, only determination.

Lastly, she responded to Jesus with reverence when He revealed Himself to her. Jesus reveals Himself to her in a very personal way by calling out her name. Hearing her name, she immediately recognized Him. She showed her reverence for Him, verbally, when she called Him, *Rabboni*. In Aramaic, the language spoken in that region, *Rabboni* literally means, "my lord/master". John uses the term, *Teacher*, for his non-Aramaic readers, and "…for the evangelist, there is no significant difference in meaning between the two terms."[3] She also showed her reverence for Him by touching Him. We get a clue that Mary was showing reverence towards Jesus by the response of the other women who had been with Mary earlier in the morning. In Matthew 28:9, these women met Jesus after Mary did and, "...they came up and took hold of His feet and worshiped Him." It appears that Mary was responding to Jesus in the same way. Jesus acknowledged Mary's adoration with this response, "Stop clinging to Me..." (vs. 17). Jesus was not concerned that she might be contaminating Him because He had not yet ascended to the Father. We see in verse 27 that Jesus invites Thomas to touch Him. Hendriksen notes, "What Jesus probably means is this: "Do you think, Mary, that by grasping hold of me so firmly (cf. Matt. 28:9), you can always keep me with you. That uninterruptible fellowship for which you yearn must wait until I have ascended to be forever with the Father."[4] Jesus would continue to have fellowship with His followers, but not in a physical way as it was when He was on the earth. "The fellowship, to be sure, would be resumed; but it would be far richer and more blessed..." with a resurrected Christ in the heavenlies.[5]

Finally, she showed her devotion to Him by being obedient. Jesus sends her to the disciples with the message, "I ascend to My Father and your Father, and My God and your God" (vs. 17).[6] It was probably easy to obey Jesus because of the overwhelming experience of physically seeing and touching the risen Jesus. We can only imagine the excitement she expressed when she announced to the disciples, "I have seen the Lord" (vs. 18). She had come to the empty tomb looking for a dead body and returned to the disciples having seen the living, resurrected Jesus.

John's response to the resurrection

John was the first disciple to arrive at the tomb after the news was reported by Mary Magdalene to the disciples that the body of Jesus was missing from the tomb. John was the first to the tomb because he was younger and could run faster than Peter. In the typical style of John, he does not identify himself in this story, but it is clearly him. This is a personal story by John that is not seen in the synoptic accounts. Perhaps this was a truly personal story that John had not revealed to anyone until he wrote this gospel account.

John gives us details about what he saw in the tomb, which indicates that this was an eye-witness account. Both John and Peter saw the grave clothes still in the tomb. This would seem rather strange if the body of Jesus had been stolen. No one would unwrap the body and leave the clothes, if they were stealing the body. This is particularly true because there had been guards outside the tomb who, because of the spectacular nature of the resurrection, had become "…like dead men" (Mt. 28:4). The guards were gone by this time, because they were reporting what had happened to the religious leaders. Another detail noted by John was the nature of the grave clothes. They were not scattered around the tomb, but appeared to be neatly in place. We can clearly infer this by his description of the face cloth which was a separate covering only for the head. John says the face cloth was, "…rolled up in a place by itself" (vs. 7). In other words, it appears the body of Jesus passed through the grave clothes without disturbing the clothes.

John, in making these observations about the grave clothes, then quickly pondered the options concerning the missing body, based upon the evidence. The only conclusion he could make, based upon these observations and recalling what Jesus said would happen, is that He did rise from the dead. John does not say all of this, but simply states, "…he saw and believed" (vs. 8). This belief by John was another step in his faith journey. We know the disciples had already believed in Jesus at the first miracle in John 2, turning the water into wine. This was a journey for each of the disciples as they grew in understanding of who Jesus was and His purpose for coming to the earth. For John, this was a mature confirmation that Jesus was, in fact, the Christ, the Son of God.

The disciples' response to the resurrection

The other disciples of Jesus were not at the same point as John was in their faith journey. John and Peter described what they saw at the tomb, but this evidence was not compelling enough for them to believe that Jesus was resurrected from the dead. They were not witnesses to the crucifixion of Jesus; therefore, they did not hear or see the amazing things that occurred while He was on the cross. Read Appendix 2 to see what grabbed John's attention when Jesus was still on the cross and its implications in John's faith journey.

Jesus was not content to wait for the disciples to meet Him in Galilee, as he had instructed the women to tell the disciples. He knew they were not ready to wait that long. Therefore, He came to them the evening after He had resurrected Himself. It is easy to imagine the shock and surprise of the disciples when Jesus appeared in their midst. The doors were locked out of fear, and suddenly, Jesus is physically present before them. This, in part, explains why the first words out of His mouth were, "Peace be with you" (vs. 19). The greeting by Jesus, *shalom*, has a greater sense than simply "Hello" to them or "Be calm from chaos." The basic idea of *shalom* is wholeness, particularly a wholeness that comes when something broken has been restored. The disciples certainly experienced that in their relationship with Jesus. They thought He was dead and gone, and now He is alive and in their midst.

Jesus also showed the disciples His hands and side as evidence of who He was and that He had been crucified. After showing them the evidence, John records that "…the disciples then rejoiced when they saw the Lord" (vs. 20). Don't forget, the disciples, excluding John, were hidden away while Jesus was being crucified and buried.

One disciple was not present when Jesus appeared to them. This disciple was Thomas, who made a statement that the other disciples had already experienced. Thomas said that the condition he needed fulfilled to believe in Jesus was physically touching Him and His wounds (vs. 25). Thomas had to wait eight days before Jesus appeared again, in the same manner as He had appeared to the other disciples. When Jesus personally invited Thomas to examine the evidence physically, Thomas believed with the famous affirmation, "My Lord and my God" (vs. 28). Even though Thomas is often ridiculed with the moniker, "Doubting Thomas", his behavior was really no different than the other disciples. Basically, Thomas was saying, "Show me the evidence and I will believe."

The miracle of the resurrection of Jesus was above and beyond the other miracles recorded in all of the four gospels. The other miracles had natural effects; the resurrection miracle had a supernatural effect. Jesus had performed a miracle that affected possibly 15,000 people for one meal, but the miracle of the resurrection of Jesus Christ affects the whole world for all time. Jesus had raised three people from the dead during His ministry, but those three people had to die again. Jesus arose from the dead by His own initiative and sits forever at the right hand of the Father.

John's purpose statement in light of this miracle

The seven miracles that John highlights points to Jesus being the Christ, the Son of God. The miracle of His resurrection from the dead validates His teachings and His purpose in coming to the earth. Many people, including ourselves, can make claims about ourselves which may be true or fabricated. The only way those claims can be validated is to prove they are true. If I said that I am the greatest pianist in the world, your response would be, "Show me." Unfortunately, my claim would collapse in a moment as soon as I touched the keyboard. For Jesus, His claims were much greater, therefore, to validate those claims would require a much higher standard. What it took was resurrecting Himself from the dead.

While Jesus was on the cross, the religious leaders were mocking Him, saying, "He saved others; He cannot save Himself" (Mt. 27:42). There was some recognition on their part that Jesus did perform miracles, but if He was who He claimed to be, then He should be able to deliver Himself from the cross. Whether they believed He performed miracles or not was irrelevant. The bottom line for these religious leaders was that they did not recognize Him as the Christ, the Son of God and they utterly rejected Him. Even after the resurrection of Jesus, they sought ways to undermine His resurrection through deceit. They bribed the guards at the tomb to spread the rumor that the disciples stole the body of Jesus and Matthew states, "…this story was widely spread among the Jews, *and is* to this day" (Mt. 28:15).

The evidence that the disciples had that Jesus had arisen from the dead was the physical evidence. They actually saw Him in person many times before He ascended into heaven. The physical evidence we have is an empty tomb in the city of Jerusalem which can be visited any time we want. The most important evidence we have is the record of His resurrection by the gospel writers and the testimony of the followers of Jesus who have experienced a transformed life because of Jesus's death, burial and resurrection.

Lessons for us from this miracle

The resurrection of Jesus anticipates what will happen at the resurrection of believers when Jesus returns. In other words, Jesus showed us by His resurrection and by revealing to us His own resurrected body, what we can expect when our time comes. He is not a ghost, but has a body recognized by those who see Him. He can also be touched and can eat food, and yet, pass through the walls of closed rooms and appear before others. Paul summarizes well what our resurrected bodies will be like in 1 Corinthians 15, "...we all will be changed, in a moment, in the twinkling of an eye...", "...The dead will be raised imperishable...", and "...this mortal must put on immortality" (vs. 51-53). The descriptions of Jesus's and our future resurrected bodies are not exhaustive, but enough is said to give us the sense that it will be amazing and fantastic.

It took physical evidence for the disciples and others to believe that He rose from the dead. Jesus had told them He would be resurrected, and when He was resurrected, they had to see Him physically to fully believe. An empty tomb was not enough. As we discussed earlier, the basis for John's belief was not the empty tomb but seeing the grave clothes lying in the tomb as though Jesus's body had been translated through the cloths.

Imagine all of the miracles and wonders these disciples witnessed, and yet, it was difficult for them to understand that He is risen. His three closest disciples had seen a glimpse of His glory on the Mount of Transfiguration (Mt. 17:1-8; Mk. 9:2-8; Lk. 9:28-36), and all of the disciples witnessed Lazarus raised from the dead a few weeks before Jesus' resurrection. You would have thought the next step of Jesus Himself rising from the dead would have been an easy step of faith, but it wasn't. It took physical evidence for them to believe.

In verse 9, John comments, "For as yet they did not understand the Scripture, that He must rise again from the dead." John states that the disciples had not pieced together the Scriptures that spoke of the Messiah rising from the dead. They needed signs to show them who He is. Remember the statement of "doubting" Thomas, who stated he would need physical evidence before he would believe (Jn. 20:25). It was not until the disciples experienced the Holy Spirit coming upon them in Acts 2 that this understanding developed, as the Holy Spirit taught them.

For the believer, 2,000 years removed from the event, we do not have the physical evidence the disciples had, but we have the record of the events in the Word of God. We also have the Holy Spirit to enlighten our hearts and help us understand the reality and significance of this event. The truth is that without the Holy Spirit, we would not understand the Scriptures to the point of believing in Christ. At this point, the disciples did not have the Holy Spirit as a teacher to enlighten their understanding of what Jesus had predicted and what the Scriptures had said. Fortunately, we have the Holy Spirit and as Jesus told Thomas, "Blessed *are* they who did not see, and *yet* believed" (Jn. 20:29).

---

[1] From Defense Casualty Analysis System, https://dcas.dmdc.osd.mil/dcas/app/conflict Casualties/ww2, Accessed 8/10/24.

[2] From https://en.wikipedia.org/wiki/Atomic_bombings_of_Hiroshima_and_Nagasaki, Accessed 8/10/24 (Note: I trust the figure from this source)

[3] Murray Harris, John in *Exegetical Guide to the Greek New Testament* (Nashville: B&H Publishing, 2015), p. 328.

[4] William Hendriksen, John in *New Testament Commentary* (Grand Rapids: Baker Academic, 1953), p. 455.

[5] Ibid, p. 455.

[6] 6 Jesus sends Mary to His disciples, in John 20:17, with a significant message, which we will briefly consider here. This message is significant because it is communicating a change in relationship between the resurrected Jesus and His disciples. There are two key points to highlight from the message. 1) Jesus calls His disciples, "…My brethren…" Jesus is describing a familial relationship He has with them, now being brothers. This is the first time Jesus has called them brothers. 2) Jesus identifies with His disciples, but is still separate from them with the statement, "…My Father and your Father, and My God and your God." In other words, they are both in relationship with the same God and Father, but the relationship Jesus has with God is different than the disciples' relationship. Jesus is the second person of the Godhead and His relationship with God is that of being of the same essence, whereas, the disciples' relationship is the mortal with the divine.

Chapter 11

WRAPPING IT UP

With an engineering and theological background, I like to organize data to make it easier to do side-by-side comparisons. This is the approach I am taking with this last chapter to provide an overview of what we have covered, develop a summary of what we have learned, and provide lessons for us to take away. This is not intended to be exhaustive but to help us remember what was covered in the previous chapters.

Comparison of references

As mentioned earlier in the book, John was written much later than the synoptic gospels. John did not need to repeat the same stories about Jesus already covered in the other books. John focused on showing his readers that Jesus was the Christ, the Son of God. Being a close disciple of Jesus, he had witnessed plenty of events from which to draw to accomplish his purpose. This is why five of the eight miracles recorded by John are unique to the Gospel of John.

Miracle	Reference in John	Reference in Synoptics
Turning water into wine	John 2: 1-11	NONE
Royal official's son healed	John 4: 46-53	NONE
The infirmed man is healed	John 5: 1-17	NONE
Feeding of the 5,000	John 6: 1-15	Mt. 14: 13-21; Mk. 6: 30-44; Lk. 9: 10-17
Jesus walking on the water	John 6: 16-21	Mt. 14: 22-33; Mk. 6: 45-52
Man, blind from birth healed	John 9: 1-34	NONE
The raising of Lazarus	John 11: 1-44	NONE

| The resurrection of Jesus | John 20: 1-29 | Mt. 28: 1-15; Mk. 16: 1- 8; Lk. 24: 1-12 |

Observations

It is easy to understand why John included the resurrection of Jesus. This was the pinnacle of miracles in terms of its significance for all of humanity. Jesus clearly shows Himself as the Christ, the Son of God. John also includes personal details in his narrative and other important details which fill in the picture of this amazing miracle.

Even though the feeding of the five thousand was recorded in all of the synoptic gospels, John saw this miracle as important, showing another level of authority exercised by Jesus and also the compassion He had for a large group of people. The details of the miracle are essentially the same among all the gospel writers, which shows the impact this miracle had on each of them and why they each chose to include it in their account.

Comparison of actions taken

In this section, the divine actions and the human actions found in each of the miracles are highlighted to show how the actions interacted with each other. When Jesus performed these miracles, He could have done everything associated with the miracle by Himself, but he had humans involved as part of the process associated with performing the miracle. For example, Jesus could have filled the waterpots, when He turned the water into wine or He could have miraculously filled the waterpots with water. Instead, He chose to use human instruments to participate in the miracle.

Miracle	Divine Action	Human Action
Turning water into wine	Jesus turns the water into wine	The servants filled the water-pots to the brim
Royal official's son healed	Jesus completely heals the boy, who was 20 miles away	The official travelled home to see his healed son
The infirmed man is healed	Jesus completely heals him and he walks	The man picked up his mat and walked
Feeding of the 5,000	Jesus multiplies the five loaves and two fish	The disciples distributed the food and then picked it up afterwards
Jesus walking on the water	Jesus walks on the water during a storm	The disciples helped Him into the boat

Man, blind from birth, healed	Jesus gives him sight through the application of a mud pack	The man washed the mud off his eyes in the Pool of Siloam
The raising of Lazarus	Jesus resuscitates him from the dead	Some men had to roll away the stone from the tomb
The resurrection of Jesus	Jesus is resurrected from the dead after three days	NONE

Observations

Most of the miracles allowed the humans who participated in them to show a level of faith in what Jesus would do. In other words, why would they join without confidence that the miracle would occur. One example of this was the man who was blind from birth. Jesus gave him specific instructions about where to go and what to do. Jesus could have healed Him on the spot, but instead, He tested his faith by giving him instructions that were not necessarily easy to complete and seemed a little crazy. After all, he had been blind from birth. In this example, the man gained his vision, and believed in Jesus.

There is a strong contrast between the resurrection of Jesus and the rest of the miracles He performed. There was no human involvement in this miracle. It was entirely a divine act. This makes sense since the second person of the Godhead not only performed the miracle, but He was also the focus of the miracle. This is another way of showing that the resurrection of Jesus was far above the other miracles in its significance and impact on the whole world, not just on a few people.

Comparison of reactions

You would have thought that the miracles of Jesus would have been so compelling that everyone who witnessed them would have believed. Unfortunately, that was not the case, and the comparison below shows a wide range of reactions to the miracles of Jesus.

Miracle	Positive Reaction	Negative Reaction
Turning water into wine	The disciples believed in Him and the guests enjoyed some great wine	None recorded
Royal official's son healed	The official and his house-hold believed in Jesus	None recorded

The infirmed man is healed	None recorded	The Jews complained about Jesus's healing on the Sabbath
Feeding of the 5,000	Full stomachs	Ready to take Jesus by force and make Him king
Jesus walking on the water	The disciples worshipped Jesus	The disciples were initially afraid when they saw Jesus
Man, blind from birth healed	The healed man believed in Jesus as the Christ	The Jews complained about Jesus's healing on the Sabbath
The raising of Lazarus	Many of the Jews believed	The Jews plotted to kill Him and to kill Lazarus
The resurrection of Jesus	Mary Magdalene, John, and the	Thomas questioned whether Jesus did rise

	disciples believed	from the dead

Observations

Even the ones who were eyewitnesses to the miracles of Jesus, had a wide variety of responses to His miracles.

- Some recognized Jesus as the Messiah and believed in Him.

- Others were taken in by the benefit derived from the miracle, but did not embrace the person who performed the miracle.

- Still others actively opposed Jesus, in spite of His miracles, and sought to have Him killed.

These responses to Jesus and His miracles are the same responses we see today when people are confronted with the person of Christ. People have not changed in two-thousand years since these miracles have occurred which makes the Bible relevant in today's world. These responses demonstrate that compelling evidence is not enough for a person to believe, because it is the human heart that primarily responds to the person of Christ.

Why this miracle

In this section, we are summarizing why John chose each of the miracles he included in his gospel account. A better way of describing this section is speculating why John chose each miracle. The last miracle, the resurrection of Jesus, does not require speculation on our part, since it validated that Jesus was the Christ, the Son of God. Otherwise, with the other miracles, we do not have the privilege of being inside John's head when he was planning and writing the story. I can also say conclusively that the Holy Spirit, who directed John in his writing, has not revealed to me, profoundly, the reason(s) for including these miracles.

Insights from the stories themselves provide the primary material for figuring this out. This material and John's purpose statement give us substantial direction.

Miracle	Why John Chose this Miracle
Turning water into wine	This miracle was done privately, primarily for the disciples, to show them, in a small way, His authority of transforming power.
Royal official's son is healed	Jesus shows His authority over disease in healing people, even when the sick person is not in Jesus's presence.
The infirmed man is healed	Jesus shows His authority to cancel the effect of sin.
Feeding of the 5,000	Jesus reveals His compassion for people by fulfilling a basic need for this huge crowd.

Jesus walking on the water	Jesus focuses on His authority to operate outside of the laws of nature.
Man blind from birth healed	Jesus heals this man, but the reactions to his healing show the heart of man in rejecting Jesus for their purposes.
The raising of Lazarus	Jesus demonstrates His authority over death as He deals with death in a deeply personal way.
The resurrection of Jesus	This is the capstone miracle that validates Jesus's teachings and works. He is the Way, the Truth, and the Life.

Observations

The miracles appear to grow in their significance as our understanding grows in knowing who Jesus is. As John presents each miracle, he does it in a context where either the miracle shows us more of who Jesus is or demonstrates what Jesus is teaching about Himself when the miracle occurs. For example, when Jesus turned the water into wine, the disciples were just beginning their journey in understanding that Jesus was the Messiah. This miracle was more subtle in nature in alignment with their understanding of Jesus. When Jesus raised Lazarus from the dead, they were witnessing a different Jesus in their understanding of Him. He is now, "…the resurrection and the life…" and they are able to see His authority over death. The miracle was much more impactful, not only to the disciples, but to those who witnessed it.

Comparison of lessons learned

This section is looking at the miracles of Jesus from a practical perspective. The focus here is not on the miracles themselves, but on what we can learn from the events that can be applied in our lives today. We can learn a lot from the people who were the recipients of the miracle or those who witnessed it.

Miracle	Lesson Learned from the Miracle
Turning water into wine	Jesus meets us where we are at in our faith journey. Jesus performed a more subtle miracle for His disciples who were new in their belief in Jesus.
Royal official's son is healed	The royal official believed Jesus healed his son, though he did not witness the miracle. Our faith should be in the One performing the miracles, not the miracles themselves.
The infirmed man is healed	If we have a distorted view of God, we will not be able to see Him as He is when He reveals Himself to us.
Feeding of the 5,000	Like the disciples, we tend to rely upon our own ingenuity to solve

	problems when we should be looking to God for help and guidance.
Jesus walking on the water	Just as Jesus has sovereign control over the big things, like weather patterns, He has control over the little things in our life. We need to be aware of His work in our lives.
Man, blind from birth healed	We witnessed the healed man's spiritual journey to faith which relates to the reality that we are also on a spiritual journey and God is guiding every step of that journey.
The raising of Lazarus	The death of a loved one is a horrible thing, and Jesus showed us by example its emotional impact. Just like Jesus, we have the freedom to mourn the loss of loved ones.
The resurrection of Jesus	What a future hope we have as followers of Christ, knowing that death has been overcome and one day we will have an eternal, incorruptible resurrection body.

Observations

We see that God meets us where we are in our journey. We don't have to be at a certain level of spirituality before

He guides us to Himself. None of us would be in the right place if it depended on us.

If we have a wrong expectation or view of God, we will not see Jesus as He really is. There is a tendency to create God in our own image, but fortunately, the Word of God shows us who Jesus is.

We must recognize that God takes care of the little and big things in our lives, if we seek Him first (see Mt. 6:33). Rather than relying upon ourselves to solve problems, we should look to God for guidance.

Conclusions

It is one thing to study Jesus's miracles and affirm that they occurred, but John's purpose in writing the Gospel of John was much greater than that. His purpose was for those reading his book to "…believe that Jesus is the Christ, the Son of God; and that believing you may have life in His name" (Jn. 20:31). We are about two thousand years removed from the writing of this book, and the purpose is still the same.

The purpose statement maintains its relevance and power because the whole world still needs to recognize that Jesus is the Christ, the Son of God and believe in His name. Each human being's need for Jesus Christ has not changed because man is still in the same spiritual state he has been since Adam and Eve sinned, when they disobeyed God. Also, the power to be transformed by the Gospel of Christ has not changed over the millennia.

Here are a couple of common denominators with all the miracles that Jesus performed:

- They happened immediately. There was not a process to the miracle developing over time. When the lame person was healed, he was immediately restored and walked. If the miracle had occurred over time, then the skeptics could attribute the miracle to something else other than Jesus's divine power.

- People benefitted from the miracles. The miracles of Jesus were not destructive in nature, but had a positive benefit. The disciples even benefited from the miracle of Jesus walking on the water. As soon as He got into the boat, they immediately found themselves at their location. We also know from other gospel accounts that He calmed the storm at the same time.

Some of you may think it would have been great to live at the time when Jesus walked the earth. It would have been a time to personally hear Jesus teach, see Him heal those who came to Him and witness Him performing miracles. The reality is that Jesus, with His teachings and doing all He did, had a very small impact when He was on the earth. His sphere of influence was confined primarily to Judea and Galilee, territories located on the outskirts of the Roman Empire. His popularity also did not extend much beyond these territories when He was physically on the earth.

Jesus's impact came after His resurrection, when He returned to heaven. Ten days after His return to heaven, the Holy Spirit came down from above, during Pentecost, as described in Acts two. Jesus told His disciples prior to His arrest, "But I tell you the truth, it is to your advantage that I go away; for if I do not go away, the Helper will not come to you; but if I go, I will send Him to you" (Jn. 16:8). This *Helper* was the Holy Spirit, who "...abides with you and will be in you" (Jn. 14:17).

At this point, Jesus's influence began to spread to the point where the gospel of Jesus Christ has now spread across the whole world and today there are hundreds of millions of genuine followers of Christ. We also have a closer relationship with Christ than the disciples had when Jesus was on the earth because the Holy Spirit indwells us. We have the teachings of Jesus written in the Word of God and we can read it whenever we desire. We may not be experiencing the healings and the miracles that Jesus performed, but we have the assurance, as followers of Christ, that we have been made whole, spiritually, through the death, burial, and resurrection of Jesus Christ.

The purpose of this book was not merely to highlight the miracles of Jesus as written in the Gospel of John. Just as John wanted his readers to believe in Jesus, this is also my desire. Learning about the miracles may expand our understanding of who Jesus is, but the final goal is that we acknowledge Jesus as the Christ who came to this earth to die for all of our sins in order to open the pathway for a restored relationship with God. This leads me to my favorite verse in the Bible, also found in the Book of John. "For God so loved the world, that he gave His only begotten Son, that whoever believes in Him shall not perish, but have eternal life" (Jn. 3:16). We can believe that Jesus performed miracles. We can personally benefit from His teachings, but ultimately, it is a life and death issue. When we believe in Jesus who died, was buried, and was resurrected from the dead, and fully committed to Him, we will have eternal life. This is what the words of Scripture offer to each one of us.

Appendix 1

WHY DON'T WE SEE MORE MIRACLES TODAY?

Is God doing miracles today? Of course He is, because He is God. I'm sure you have heard of stories where a person had a disease that completely disappeared and the doctors were baffled because the person was healed and they could not find any trace of the disease. This is a miracle because the natural laws that dictate the characteristics of the disease would not have led to a complete healing. Even though there are miracles today, this does not mean that God intends for miracles to be normative.

God intended for miracles to be uncommon, special, and with a purpose in mind. In the Gospel of John, we get a hint that miracles were not commonplace. In the story of the man who gained his sight after being blind from birth (John 9), the healed man makes an interesting comment to the Pharisees about his own miracle. He said to them, "Since the beginning of time it has never been heard that anyone opened the eyes of a person born blind. If this man were not from God, He could do nothing" (vs. 32-33). This man recognized the rarity of a blind man being healed. This made it clear to him that the healing had to be from God and the miracle was performed by someone who came from God. This healing showed the man that Jesus was the Christ and he believed (Jn. 9:38).

Miracles in Biblical history

We see a clustering of miracles in only three places in the Bible. These groups of miracles were at pivotal points in God's history of His people:

- God delivered the children of Israel out of Egypt and their trek in the wilderness. This clearly was a significant period in the history of God's people, Israel. God used Moses and Aaron as His instruments to "persuade" the Pharoah of Egypt to let His people leave the land. God brought destructive miracles upon the land of Egypt to get Pharoah's attention and he finally succumbed to God's plan. Miracles also occurred during the forty years the children of Israel were in the wilderness. God provided them protection, guidance and provision.

Amazingly, the provision (manna) stopped when they entered the Promised Land.

- The time of the prophets Elijah and Elisha. These two prophets lived in the northern kingdom of Israel, and they were the LORD's spokesmen to the apostate kings and people of the kingdom. Some of the miracles during this time were public, others were private, and one miracle was the healing of a man who was an enemy of Israel. As the nation turned to Baal, God used miracles through Elijah and Elisha to show the people that the LORD was their God. Unfortunately, the nation of Israel did not turn to the LORD, and they were invaded by the Assyrians and taken into captivity.

- The life and ministry of Jesus Christ and the church's beginnings as described in the Book of Acts. We have spent this whole book looking at Jesus' miracles and the importance they played in His ministry. Miracles continued in the early church, as seen in the Book of Acts, to demonstrate God's supernatural hand on the church as it was being established.

In the last days, when Christ returns, as described in the Book of Revelation, we will see another group of miracles. In those days, false miracles will be performed by Satan's servants for the sole purpose of deceiving the world. On the other hand, miracles will be performed by God to counter Satan's deceptions.

The frequency of miracles today

Here are some reasons why miracles are less frequent today than what was during certain periods of Biblical history:

- God is not capricious and is not trying to be a "showman" before humanity. God does not perform miracles just to show mankind that He is God and that He can do whatever He wants. This would degrade the God of the universe to the level of the Greek and Roman gods, who liked to show off their power to inflate their egos. When God performs a miracle, there is a purpose behind it, which may have a positive or negative impact. Most of the miracles performed in Egypt during the time of Moses, were destructive to get Pharoah's attention. Ultimately, it had a positive impact. The children of Israel were allowed to leave Egypt.

- Excessive miracles would undermine the predictability of the universe. The laws of the universe allow us to see an orderly God who created those laws. These natural laws also allow us to develop science and have a basic understanding of the universe. This opens the doors to practically developing ways we can use the laws for creating technology. If miracles frequently disrupted the laws of the universe, then the laws would lack the predictability we expect. We would have technologies we could not rely upon, because the laws upon which those technologies are based are unpredictable.

- We should walk by faith, not by sight. If miracles are frequent, we will tend to rely upon the miracles rather than our faith in God. If you recall from the miracle of the feeding of the five thousand, there were some who were ready to take Jesus to Jerusalem and make Him king (Jn. 6:15). What was their motivation in making Him king? The miracles He performed benefitted them and they wanted a Messiah who would provide for them. They were focused on the miracles and not on the one who performed the miracle. God intends for us to trust in Him because of who He is and not rely upon His miracles.

- God has given us the Word of God to understand who He is, what He has done in history, and what He will be doing. We do not need miracles for Jesus to show us He is the Christ, the Son of God. He has already done this and it is recorded in the Word of God. We are so privileged to have the completed Word of God in our hands to see what He has done and to recognize that He is the same God today as He was when the Scriptures were written. He may not be doing the miracles today that we read about in the Scriptures, but He is still an all-powerful and faithful God.

- God doesn't need to do miracles now, but He does do them. This follows up from the previous point that God has given us the completed Word of God to show us who He is and His plan for the world. The miracles that were performed during certain periods of Biblical history had purposes in mind, highlighting, on a grand scale, what God was doing through His people. We are in a period of history where we are awaiting the return of Christ and the next period of miracles during the last days.

- Finally, let me make the point again. I am not saying that God is not doing miracles today. God is at work and He can do whatever He pleases whenever He wants to. I don't have any data to quantify how many miracles are happening around the world today and what the trends are with miracles. What I can say is that we have seen and will see a time when a cluster of miracles will reveal a significant period in God's grand plan for the world.

Perhaps the greatest miracle of all

Would we consider an individual today, repenting of his sins and coming to Christ as his Savior, a miracle? Yes, but not in the same sense as we have seen with physical miracles. In a spiritual sense, it is a miracle because a person who is spiritually dead is made alive in Christ. When death is spoken of in the Bible, it has the idea of separation. When a person is physically dead, their soul is separated from their physical body. When a person is spiritually dead, their soul is separated from God.

As we saw in John 11, Lazarus was physically raised from the dead. This would be considered a miracle because it is impossible for a person to rise from the dead, especially after being dead for four days. Apart from the laws of nature being changed, this person could not be made alive again. When Lazarus died, his soul was separated from his body. When Jesus brought him back to life, his soul was reunited with his body. In the same way, a person who is spiritually dead, is physically alive, but his soul is separated from God because of his sin. This person cannot be made alive spiritually apart from the work of the Holy Spirit drawing this person to Christ. The person becomes spiritually alive when the relationship between God and that person's soul is restored, as God intended it to be. We cannot make ourselves alive spiritually through some work on our part because we are dead, and that is the nature of being dead.

Paul makes this point very clear in chapter two of the book of Ephesians. He begins the chapter by telling the Ephesians their spiritual state before Christ. "And you were dead in your offences and sins, in which you previously walked according to the course of this world…" (vs. 1-2). They were physically alive, but spiritually dead because they were spiritually separated from God. They were dead men walking. After discussing the nature of being dead spiritually, Paul talks about the process of being made alive with Christ. "But God, being rich in mercy, because of His great love with which He loved us, even when we were dead in our wrongdoings, made us alive together with Christ…" (vs. 4-5). This passage tells us how we are made alive. It is a work of God because of the work of Christ on the cross. The conclusion is that dead people, whether physically or spiritually, cannot be made alive apart from God bringing them to life.

Being made alive spiritually, after being spiritually dead, is an even more amazing event than Lazarus being raised by Jesus. The big difference between the two events is that Lazarus had to die again. Technically, he was resuscitated only to die again at some point in his life. When we are made spiritually alive, the result is eternal life. We will never be spiritually dead again because of the efficacy of Christ's work on the cross. This is a miracle! We once were dead and are now alive.

Appendix 2

JOHN 19:31-37
SO THAT YOU MAY BELIEVE

The darkest day in history took place two thousand years ago, when Jesus Christ, the second person of the Godhead, was crucified on the cross. Imagine the pain and despair the disciples experienced as they saw their Messiah killed. It was only later that they understood the significance of His death--for the sins of the world.

In the midst of John's description of the crucifixion and death of Jesus, John makes a strange declaration around the death of Christ. He speaks in emphatic terms about the veracity of an eyewitness to the death of Jesus. In John 19:35, he states, "And he who has seen has testified, and his testimony is true; and he knows that he is telling the truth, so that you also may believe." John wants you to know there is an eyewitness who saw Jesus die and we can trust this testimony. Why is this so important to John? The last phrase of the verse tells us why, "…so that you also may believe."

We know the theme of showing that Jesus is the Christ was important to John. In his purpose statement for the book (John 20:30-31), John states that he wants to show you, the reader, that Jesus is the Christ so that you might believe and have eternal life. He primarily showed that Jesus is the Christ through recording key signs (miracles) that Jesus performed during His earthly ministry. Now, John is highlighting that the death of Christ can also point you toward faith in Him.

John points out two details around Christ's death that lead to his eyewitness verification. The first detail revolves around the "premature" death of Christ. Jesus died on His own terms and stated so when He cried out, "It is finished." The work on the cross was complete, and Jesus, "…gave up His spirit." From the Roman soldier's perspective, this was unusual. Crucifixion was intended to be a long and agonizing means of death. This meant the condemned person could last for days on the cross before he would expire. Jesus was on the cross for only six hours. This "premature" death on the part of Jesus even surprised Pilate. When Joseph of Arimathea came and asked for the body of Jesus, Matthew records in Matthew 15:44, "Pilate wondered if He was dead by this time, and summoning the centurion, he questioned him as to whether He was already dead."

John records that the Jews wanted the three condemned men removed from their crosses before the Sabbath began (vs. 31), therefore, the Roman soldiers broke the legs of the two criminals who were still alive. This sped up the process and they quickly expired. With their legs broken, they could not support their bodies, which restricted their breathing. This led them to die by asphyxiation. The soldiers did not have to break Jesus' legs because He was already dead.

The second detail that John includes in his account of Jesus's death is the soldier piercing the side of Jesus with a spear (vs. 34). John does not record why the soldier decided to pierce the side of Jesus, but he does describe what happened when Jesus was pierced; "…immediately blood and water came out." There have been modern medical explanations of this phenomenon, but in John's mind, it was a verification that Jesus was, in fact, dead.

With these details pointed out, John now takes an aside from the narrative (vs. 35-37) to explain why these details are important. He explains in verses 37-38 that these two details were the fulfilment of a foreshadowing[1] and a prophecy concerning the Christ. John quotes from Exodus 12:46, concerning bones not being broken and from Zechariah 12:10, concerning His piercing. John translated both of these verses from the Hebrew Old Testament. I mention this detail because there is another verse, Psalm 34:20, which mentions bones not broken. John used the

Exodus passage, a more literal translation of the Hebrew text.

The first fulfilment of the circumstances around Jesus's death is found in Exodus 12:46. This passage is contained in the context of the first Passover, where it speaks of the Passover lamb. The passage says, "It [the Passover lamb] is to be eaten in a single house; you are not to bring forth any of the flesh outside, nor are you to break any bone of it." Clearly, John is associating Jesus with the Passover lamb, which was sacrificed and its blood was used to protect the family from the death angel. It is no coincidence that Jesus was crucified at Passover as "...the Lamb of God who takes away the sin of the world" (John 1:29). John recognized the Passover lamb as a foreshadow of Jesus and He fulfilled that role as an unblemished lamb without any broken bones to be sacrificed for the whole world.

The second fulfillment, highlighted by John, is quoted from Zechariah 12:10. This prophetic passage, speaking of the coming Messiah (Christ), says "...so they will look on Me whom they have pierced; and they will mourn for Him..." When Jesus Christ returns, one of the ways the Jews will recognize Him is by the pierced wound in His side. Even in the next chapter of John, the disciple Thomas says he will not believe in the risen Jesus unless I, "...put my hand into His side..." (John 20:25). Amazingly, Jesus accommodated Thomas, when He appeared to His disciples, and encouraged Thomas to put his hand into His pierced side. What was Thomas's response? "My Lord and my God" (vs. 28). The spear wound in the side of Jesus was another sign that He was the Christ.

John was so adamant about the veracity of these events at Jesus's death because these events were foretold and literally fulfilled by Jesus. A detail to note is that the foreshadowing and prophecy were fulfilled after Jesus had died. Humanly speaking, He could not "manipulate" the situation to make sure none of His bones were broken and His side was pierced. God the Father orchestrated these events to demonstrate again that Jesus was the Christ, the Savior of the world. John wanted to make sure his audience understood this so that they "…may believe that Jesus is the Christ, the Son of God; and that believing you may have life in His name" (John 20:31).

It is obvious that these details around the death of Jesus were important enough to be included in his gospel account. How should these details impact us as followers of Christ? From an apologetics perspective, these details add to the argument that Jesus was who He said He was. Matthew was the gospel writer who focused on showing Jesus as the Messiah as prophesied in the Old Testament. John reinforced Matthew's argument with these small details around the death of Jesus.

From a theological perspective, these details show the sovereignty of God at work in orchestrating all of these small details. What an assurance it gives us that God is also orchestrating the small events in our lives. Just as He had a plan and purpose in Jesus becoming flesh and dwelling among us, so also God has a plan and purpose for our lives. These details presented by John should reinforce our faith in Jesus as our Messiah and Savior. These details should also reinforce our faith in God as a loving Heavenly Father whose concern for us is shown, down to the details of our lives.

ADDENDUM

A final question you may ask in closing is this: Who was this person that John described as witnessing the crucifixion? It is generally acknowledged that John was referring to himself. It is not unusual, in his gospel account, to refer to himself indirectly. One example of this is in John 13:23, where John states, "There was reclining on Jesus's bosom one of His disciples, whom Jesus loved." John was referring to himself as the one reclining next to Jesus. John even uses this exact phrase in John 21:20 when Jesus spends time with the disciples at the Sea of Galilee. The clincher that John was referring to himself is found in John 21:24 when he records, "This is the disciple who is testifying to these things and wrote these things, and we know that his testimony is true." This statement is very similar to what he states in John 19:35.

---

[1] The term foreshadowing is used in the text above relative to the Passover lamb being a foreshadowing of Jesus. Rather than discuss what foreshadowing meant above and perhaps cause confusion about the point being made, I decided to defer until now to explain what I mean by foreshadowing. Foreshadowing is defined by dictionary.com as "an indication of something that will happen in the future, often used as a literary device to hint at or allude to future

plot." In other words, something has happened in the past that points to something that has or will occur in the future.

Foreshadowing is what the Passover lamb was concerning Jesus. The Passover lamb has its meaning in the context in which Passover was originally celebrated and how Passover is celebrated by Jews today. The Passover lamb also points to Jesus because He acted as an unblemished Passover lamb when He was crucified on the cross.

In biblical interpretation, this foreshadowing described above is called typology. Here is a definition of typology by Donald Campbell that says it well, "an Old Testament institution, event, person, object or ceremony which has reality and purpose in biblical history, but which also by divine design foreshadows something yet to be revealed" (The Interpretation of Type, *Bibliotheca Sacra*, Vol. 112, no. 447, p. 250). In the case of the Passover lamb, it would be the type that is real and stands alone in its historical context. Jesus would be the antitype as He adds richness and a depth of meaning to the type. The Apostle Paul makes it very clear that Jesus is the antitype when he says in 1 Corinthians 5:7, "For Christ our Passover also has been sacrificed".

Bibliography

Campbell, DK 1955. The Interpretation of Types, *Bibliotheca Sacra*, Vol. 112, no. 447, pp. 249-257.

Harris, MJ 2015. John, *Exegetical Guide to the Greek New Testament*. Nashville: B&H Publishing.

Hendriksen, W 1953. John, *New Testament Commentary*. Grand Rapids: Baker Academic.

Lattourette, KS 1975. *A History of Christianity*. Peabody, MA: Prince Press.

Schürer, E 1890. *A History of the Jewish People in the Time of Jesus Christ*. Peabody, MA: Hendrickson Publishers.

Spicq, C 1994. *Theological Lexicon of the New Testament*. Peabody, MA: Hendrickson Publishers.

vonWahlde, UC 2011. The Puzzling Pool of Bethesda, Biblical Archaeology Review, September/October. https://library.biblicalarchaeology.org/article/the-puzzling-pool-of-bethesda/. Accessed 7/13/24.

Wood BG, 2023. Extraordinary Excavations: The Pilgrimage Road and the Pool of Siloam, created November 7, https://biblearchaeology.org/research/chronological-categories/life-and-ministry-of-jesus-and-apostles/5107-extraordinary-excavations-the-pilgrimage-road-and-the-pool-of-siloam. Accessed 8/11/24

About Kharis Publishing:

Kharis Publishing, an imprint of Kharis Media LLC, is a leading Christian and inspirational book publisher based in Aurora, Chicago metropolitan area, Illinois. Kharis' dual mission is to give voice to under-represented writers (including women and first-time authors) and equip orphans in developing countries with literacy tools. That is why, for each book sold, the publisher channels some of the proceeds into providing books and computers for orphanages in developing countries so that these kids may learn to read, dream, and grow. For a limited time, Kharis Publishing is accepting unsolicited queries for nonfiction (Christian, self-help, memoirs, business, health and wellness) from qualified leaders, professionals, pastors, and ministers. Learn more at:
 https://kharispublishing.com/

www.ingramcontent.com/pod-product-compliance
Lightning Source LLC
Chambersburg PA
CBHW070150100426
42743CB00013B/2871